From Catholic to Protestant

introductions to history

Series Editor: David Birmingham,
Professor of Modern History, University of Kent at Canterbury

A series initiated by members of the School of History at the
University of Kent at Canterbury

From Catholic to Protestant

Religion and the people in Tudor England

Doreen Rosman
University of Kent

First published in 1996 by UCL Press

UCL Press Limited
University College London
Gower Street
London WC1E 6BT

and
1900 Frost Road, Suite 101
Bristol
Pennsylvania 19007-1598

The name of University College London (UCL) is a registered
trade mark used by UCL Press with the consent of the owner.

British Library Cataloguing in Publication Data
A catalogue record for this book is available from the British Library.

ISBN: 1-85728-433-X PB

Typeset in Sabon and Gill Sans.
Printed and bound by
Bookcraft (Bath) Ltd.

Contents

To Peter, Rose, Mark and Hannah

Preface

This book is designed for people who are interested in studying the religious changes of the sixteenth century but find the mentality of Tudor people hard to comprehend. Why were young artisans and labourers prepared to face death by burning rather than deny their faith? Why did new regulations about the dress worn by ministers of religion prompt a London mob to riot? The chapters that follow attempt to describe what people believed in a way that may be comprehensible to twentieth-century readers who do not have any religious background. Faith was not just an intellectual matter: we need to try to get into people's feelings, to understand what their beliefs meant to them. In the sixteenth century deep passions were evoked by issues that seem to us petty, unimportant or even incomprehensible. This book aims to help students enter into the mind-set and experience of the people they are studying, to understand their emotions, their framework of thought and the world in which they lived. It tries to explore what it felt like to live through the religious changes of the Tudor period and assesses the impact these had upon everyday life.

CHAPTER ONE

Religion and daily life
in the early sixteenth century

Five hundred years ago the church was part of the fabric of everyday life in a way it has long ceased to be. Wherever people looked they saw religious symbols. At parish boundaries, at street crossings, at stiles and on bridges, carved crosses and statues of saints proclaimed that God was guarding those who lived there and travellers who journeyed through. The year was structured round religious festivals, not just Christmas and Easter, which survive as public holidays today, but many others commemorating key episodes in the life of Jesus and the birth of the church. Interspersed among the major festivals were vast numbers of saints' days. These constituted the most commonly recognized calendar in a largely unlettered age: people planning to meet or fixing a date by which a debt might be paid made arrangements with reference to Peter's-tide, the Eve of St Agnes, or the fair that met on a particular saint's day. On important holy days (the origin of holidays) work ceased or was substantially reduced so that people could attend religious services, feasts, revels and sports. During some festivals, pageants and plays on biblical themes were performed at different venues within each town. Often there were street parades, with accompanying handbells, banners and processional crosses.

This chapter aims to outline the belief system that lay behind these practices and to explain how people thought. This is not to imply that belief was uniform: the last section will attempt to explore the diversity of religious attitudes. But early modern people shared widespread assumptions that are alien to our society: this chapter seeks to elucidate those assumptions and communicate something of what it felt like to hold such beliefs.

1

Beliefs and practices

In the early sixteenth century belief was a corporate and not just a personal matter. Religious rituals were an expression of communal solidarity, ways of securing the welfare of the community. This was most clearly demonstrated at rogationtide when parishioners marched round the boundaries of their parish, demarcating them by hitting the ground with sticks. This affirmed their right to land that might otherwise be claimed by neighbouring communities. The rogationtide marchers believed that the security of their community depended not just on relationships with bordering parishes but on God's favour and protection. A major function of the rite was to beseech his blessing on the newly planted crops. (The word "rogation" derives from the Latin verb to ask, *rogare*.) It was also designed to drive out evil spirits that might hinder growth or destroy neighbourliness. The devil, an evil force opposed to God, was believed constantly to watch for opportunities of disturbing the peace, of harming the unwary, and of distracting Christians from trust in God. Vividly depicted on wall-paintings and woodcuts, he was very much part of popular consciousness. At rogationtide an image of a dragon was carried round some parishes, its long cloth tail docked on the final day of the festival to show that diabolic power could not ultimately prevail against that of God.

The cosmic battle between God and the devil was believed to go back to the beginning of time. Human lives were part of the battleground. Misled by the devil, the first human beings had turned away from their creator as did all later generations. God had sent his son, Jesus Christ, to earth to share human life and bring sinful people back to him. Over the centuries many different theories had been put forward about how this was achieved. John Bossy has summarized what the Church taught around 1500, a set of beliefs that reflect the corporate nature of people's thinking. When offence had been given, compensation had to be paid, but this need not be done by the individual concerned; kin could pay instead. (In outlying parts of Europe clans still demanded restitution for harm done to their own members from the community of those who had wronged them.) When Jesus died on a cross he was standing in for his kin; his death was offered to God as redress for the offence caused by the disobedience of the rest of humankind (Bossy 1985: 3–6).

What Christ had done was re-enacted every time "Mass", the central act of Christian worship, was celebrated. Congregations watched as priests raised wafer bread and wine aloft: these were symbols of the broken body and spilt blood of Jesus. But they were more than mere symbols for at the moment of elevation the bread and wine were believed to be transformed into that body and blood. To receive the bread or "host" at these "communion" services was a particularly important religious act, a way of communing with God. At most services the people only watched, but it was widely assumed that merely to be present brought one closer to God. To see him in this, his chosen form, was to draw near to his power. The great feast of Corpus Christi, honouring the body of Christ offered in the Mass, was one of the most enthusiastically supported festivals of the year. The one occasion on which ordinary people regularly received the host at communion was Easter Sunday, the celebration of Jesus' rising from the dead. During the season of Lent, the 40 days before Easter, diets had been restricted as a reminder of Christ's suffering. On Easter Day parishioners, who had shared the common Lenten discipline, broke their fast together as they received communion. In so doing they affirmed that they were at peace with God and with each other.

Before receiving the host, people were expected to confess their sins to a priest, thereby admitting their wrongdoing to God. As a sign of their penitence they had to perform acts of penance, which generally took the form of set prayers and alms-giving. Having pronounced the penance, the priest laid his hand on the person's head and declared God's forgiveness in an act of absolution. Absolved from sin, penitents were reconciled to God, and, if dying, were ready to receive communion and other rites of the church prior to meeting their maker.

Death was an ever-present reality. It could not be distanced or largely ignored as tends to happen today, and so it was integrated into people's understanding of life. Instead of being seen as an end, death was regarded as part of a continuum, a staging-post on a journey that continued after life on this earth had ceased. What happened after death was graphically depicted in "doom paintings", a dominant feature of many churches. These huge murals portrayed the Last Judgement at the close of time when all would be consigned either to heaven or to hell. Christ was the central figure in most doom paintings: he was portrayed seated in majesty, his hands, scarred by the nails of crucifixion, raised in judgement and blessing. To his left was depicted the fate of those who had continued in wickedness, scorning

Christian teaching or impenitently indulging in the seven deadly sins of pride, covetousness, lust, envy, gluttony, anger and sloth. Nimble, gloating demons were poised, pitchforks ready, to hurl the great and the destitute, proud church officials and obdurate heretics, down into the gaping mouth of hell. On his right those whom Christ had redeemed were shown rising naked from their graves, watched by smiling, trumpet-bearing angels who waited to escort them to the ramparts of the heavenly kingdom.

In addition to heaven and hell, the church taught that there was an intermediate state of purgatory which those destined for heaven entered as soon as they died. Christ's mercy was such that even the most depraved person who repented could ultimately expect to be received into bliss. First, however, fallible human beings had to be made fit for life with God. One function of purgatory was to cleanse and to purify. In English thought greater emphasis was placed on its other, more retributive, purpose. Forgiveness did not preclude penalties for the forgiven sinner still had debts to pay. The acts of penance which penitents performed each time they went to confession were not only signs to God that they really were sorry; they were also ways of making amends for their wrongdoing. The idea of purgatory had developed in the course of the Middle Ages because most people were not in a position to offer God adequate recompense for their failure to live in his way. It provided an opportunity after death for people to pay penalties which penance had not fully satisfied on earth.

Since purgatory was a place of pain it was desirable to ensure that the time spent there was as short as possible. One obvious step was to make as much restitution to God as possible before death. Giving to the poor and endowing religious foundations were recognized ways of paying one's debt; by so doing the avaricious learnt to control their greed. Prayers, attendance at extra Masses, and pilgrimages to shrines of saints were also acceptable offerings; these fostered devotion and a God-centred frame of mind. From the mid-fourteenth century "indulgences" began to be granted to those who performed these acts. The pope (the head of the church) or his representative confirmed that by going on a particular pilgrimage, by saying certain prayers, by contributing funds to a new church, an individual would gain remission, specified in terms of days or years, from the expected sentence in purgatory. However alien this may seem to modern minds, the emotions involved may not have been radically different from those which operate today. The desire to know that effort will be rewarded was no doubt as strong in the past as it is now, and indulgences catered for this need. They reassured people that their endeavours to avoid future suffering would bear fruit.

Indulgences were not designed to operate mechanically: in the eyes of the church authorities, penitence was essential. The pope's confirmation that the performance of specified acts reduced time in purgatory was meant to encourage piety. Instructions in prayer books stressed that prayers had to be said with inner devotion if the indulgences attached to them were to be obtained. But inevitably practice degenerated: some Christians doubtless assumed that mere repetition was enough; others probably contributed to charity to gain an indulgence with scant regard for the cause they were supporting. That they were willing to do so shows how strong a hold purgatory had on popular imagination.

Another way of shortening time in purgatory was through prayers for the dead. Many chantries were built. These were chapels, often inside a church, in which Masses were regularly sung (hence *chant*ry) for the soul of the founder. People making wills frequently set aside sums of money to pay a priest to offer a specified number of Masses, at which prayers would be said for their souls. Many joined guilds or fraternities, one of whose functions was to cater for members' needs after death. The guild ensured that prayers were regularly said for the repose of the dead person's soul and often took responsibility for providing a funeral. Each craft had its own guild but in addition there were many fraternities operating at most levels of society, open to men and women of any craft and none. New ones were regularly formed and some people belonged to several. Much of the socio-religious festivity of late medieval England was organized by the guilds.

The guilds are a good illustration of the communal nature of society. Some imposed strict moral codes on their members; most required them to perform certain duties such as attending the annual guild Mass and feast, and the funerals of fellow members. Guilds were mutual insurance societies both for this life and for that to come. Their funds were used to provide benefits to members who suffered disaster or destitution. Living members of guilds prayed for the souls of those who had passed on, knowing that others in turn would pray for them. Just as Christ had compensated for the wrongdoing of his kin by dying on the cross, so members of the surrogate family of the guild offered reparation to God in the form of prayers for the sins of fellow members.

The sense of kin and community transcended the grave. The dead were seen as part of society and were sometimes enrolled retrospectively as members of guilds so that surviving members could take responsibility for their after-death needs. Those who worshipped in parish churches were surrounded by mementos of their predecessors. Many of the decorative items that enhanced worship were gifts of previous parishioners, for whose souls those still living were regularly invited to pray. Any offering, however small, ensured that the donor's name was inscribed on the bede roll, a list of benefactors that was read out once a year, a clear affirmation that the parish community extended both sides of the permeable barrier of death.

Members of the wider community of faithful souls were also commemorated in the local church. There were paintings and carvings of Mary the mother of Jesus, the disciples and early fathers of the church. Statues of saints were wedged into every nook and cranny. When people asked the saints to pray for them they were addressing not abstractions but men and women of whom they had a clear visual image. As the prayers of the living could aid the dead, so the prayers of those in heaven could affect the wellbeing of those on earth. Just as they might choose to consult appropriate specialists on earth, so people approached saints who were believed to be sympathetic towards particular ills. St Erasmus who was disembowelled understood the distress of bowel complaints; St Apollonia who was tortured by having her teeth knocked out was an obvious source of appeal for sufferers from toothache. As on earth, supplicants sought help from someone with whom they had connections or felt particularly at ease, the patron saint of their guild or church, or the saint by whose statue they regularly knelt. Saints seemed more accessible than a holy God who, like an earthly potentate, was best approached through intermediaries. It was assumed that requests were more likely to be granted if they were made by those who had already gained God's approval.

Part of the appeal of the saints was that they offered hope of protection and healing in a world in which women and men were constantly at risk from ills they could do little to avert: childbirth, disease and plague. Christians who had lived holy lives became channels through which God's power might pass to others. Desperate people whose existence was made intolerable by harrowing illness or handicap limped, crawled or were led to shrines of saints all over England, leaving wax models of themselves and wax replicas of the afflicted parts of their bodies as offerings. That crutches were also left suggests that some at least found relief from their suffering.

How people thought

To understand these beliefs we need to recognize that awareness of the supernatural was very much part of everyday life. Miracles were regularly proclaimed. The finding of lost possessions, recovery from sickness, resumption of egg-laying by hens were all attributed to saintly intervention, showing how closely the supernatural was integrated with the natural in popular thought. The modern tendency to segregate sacred and secular would have seemed most strange to early sixteenth-century people, for God, the devil, and their respective squadrons were believed to be busily at work in the world.

This meant that religious and worldly concerns were inextricably linked. It is inappropriate to ask whether something was done for religious or secular reasons because people at the time would not have made that distinction. Financing a chantry chapel was a statement of social status and a reflection of religious concern. Guilds served both a religious and a socio-economic function. A man might become a member of a religious order, entering a monastery for the rest of his life, both to gain security and to serve God through a life of prayer. Medieval people did not need psychoanalysts to tell them about multiple motives; this was part of the God-given nature of the world. By his beneficent arrangement any one action could serve a multiplicity of purposes. Pilgrimages were fun and a means of benefiting one's soul. Religious festivals were an expression of belief and a way of enjoying oneself which could involve getting drunk. People were not embarrassed as some of their descendants have been by the juxtaposition of bawdiness and piety in the mystery (trade) plays performed by craft guilds during religious festivals: the holy was not curtained off from the rest of life but integrated with it. When making his will, one man

saw the community drink as an opportunity to have prayers said for his soul. He left three acres of meadow and one acre of arable to hold "one drynkynge evermore to be kept the twysday in the rogacon weke at Pekworth Crosse to the Intent to be prayd for ever more and to be parte taker of prayers and suffragis there sayd" (Hanawalt 1986: 260).

"His bequest", Barbara Hanawalt concludes, "would have provided a generous quantity of beer."

If secular and sacred were integrated so too were the material and the spiritual. By becoming a human being Christ had shown that supernatural power could operate through things earthly and temporal. It was believed that such power was particularly focused in certain holy objects, most obviously the consecrated bread and wine, but also candles and water that had been blessed by priests for ritual purposes, and a multiplicity of relics: bones from saints' bodies, fragments of the cross on which Christ died, and even drops of his blood. Pilgrimages were made to centres where relics were housed, and on appropriate commemorative days, safely encased in decorative caskets, they were paraded round the streets for popular veneration.

The reverence accorded to such things reminds us that people invested both objects and words with greater power than we do. Sacred objects and holy words were crucial weapons in the battle that was constantly waged between good and evil, God and the devil. Since all human beings were born in sin, it was important that newborn children were brought quickly under the protection of Christ by being "baptized". This meant that the baby was immersed in holy water and marked by the sign of the cross: "do not dare to violate, o cursed devil", announced the officiating priest, "this sign of the holy cross which we now make on her forehead" (quoted, Duffy 1992: 280). The water, the gesture and the prayer were more than mere symbols; in the eyes of those watching they created a cordon of protection around the vulnerable child. People regularly made the sign of the cross on their breasts and foreheads. At rogationtide the processional cross was taken into the fields, since its physical presence was believed to bring blessing to the corn. At the same time extracts from the Gospels were recited over the newly sown crops, for certain passages of scripture were conceived to be particularly powerful weapons against evil.

Objects could operate as proxies for the presence of their owners. To light candles in front of statues of saints was to leave some mark of oneself in their presence, identifying donors with the prayers that were being offered even when unable to be present. Objects associated with saints carried their power to those in need: in some parishes women were able to borrow lying-in girdles linked to particular saints to see them through the dangers of childbirth. Since power inhered in objects, placing oneself in the vicinity of or even touching the relic of a saint was likely to be more effective than prayer alone.

In a partially literate society belief was expressed by tangible and visible means as well as by the written and spoken word. The liturgy or order of service of the church was highly dramatic, using action and symbol to retell and re-enact the message of the Gospels. At Candlemas, 2 February, parishioners processed with lighted candles round the church, commemorating the occasion when the infant Christ was greeted in the temple as "a light to lighten the Gentiles", a light that the forces of darkness could not overcome. The candles were believed to provide protection against evil. Jesus' triumphal entry into Jerusalem was celebrated on the Sunday before Easter by processions round the churchyard with the congregation waving branches reminiscent of the palms with which welcoming crowds had strewn his way. These "palms" were burnt and the ashes from them daubed on people's foreheads at the start of the next Lent (Ash Wednesday) as a sign of penitence and a reminder that human beings come from and return to dust. "Creeping to the cross" was a common Good Friday ritual: as Christ had staggered through the streets of Jerusalem carrying his cross, so worshippers went forward barefoot and on their knees to kiss the foot of the cross. At the end of the day the cross was wrapped in linen cloths, like the body once removed from it, and "buried" with the host in a special Easter sepulchre; parishioners watched over this until Easter morning when the cross was triumphantly raised and carried round the church in celebration of the resurrection. Through the symbolic actions of church services, a community that could not read was familiarized with the stories and teaching of the Bible.

The images with which churches abounded served the same function. The mellow greyness we associate with medieval churches does not reflect their appearance in their prime for roofs and walls were often brightly painted; pictures and motifs, carvings and sculpture were displayed all round the building, each telling their own story. Above and around the great central arch there was often a doom painting. Beneath it was a "rood screen", a wood or stone partition, carved or painted with images of saints, and surmounted by a great crucifix (the rood). This carving of the dying Christ upon the cross, flanked by images of his mother and St John, was a constant reminder at the focal point of the church of the central tenet of the Christian faith.

It is important to realize that these images were not mere illustrations of the biblical message. They were themselves primary means of communication. Drawing on the writings of Reginald Pecock, a fifteenth-century Bishop of Chichester, Margaret Aston comments

> Sight was the highest of the senses, seeing better than hearing . . . He [Pecock] explained how much less painful and laborious it was to learn the outline of a story from a visual depiction than from a text . . . As long as it was taken for granted that reading necessitated hearing (muttering or mouthing, if not vocalizing the word on the page) the speed of comprehension was naturally slow: slower than it is for those whose familiarity with letters is such that the written (or printed) words themselves become electric signals, direct referents of reality, more nearly comparable to the painted depiction (Aston 1984: 116–17).

Words had their place, but they were one form of communication among many. At the very least people were likely to know by heart a few basic prayers, the *Paternoster* (Lord's Prayer) and the *Ave* (Hail Mary). While services were in Latin, sermons were preached in English occasionally by parish priests and more regularly by friars, members of preaching orders, who travelled the country addressing the people on religious matters. Devotional books were becoming available in increasing numbers. But these were not necessarily treated as books are today. Eamon Duffy has suggested that the 57,000 primers or prayer books produced for lay use in the fifteenth and early sixteenth centuries were essentially holy objects. They were often illustrated with pictures of the suffering Christ and of saints, the sentences profusely punctuated with signs of the cross. Since the text was in Latin many purchasers would be able only partially to comprehend what was written, but the opening phrases of prayers familiar from the liturgy would alert them to the main tenor of the words. The text was less a source of communication than a means of invoking divine power. "Holy words" did not need to be understood for benefit to accrue. Devout readers, who brooded on the pictures in their primers as they recited words of memorized prayers, possessed in their homes visual aids to devotion very similar to those which they saw all around them in their churches (Duffy 1992: 210–32).

Diversity and uniformity

Eamon Duffy's (1992) wide-ranging and enlightening account of "traditional religion in England", to which this chapter is indebted, has been criticized for implying that everyone shared the same beliefs and patterns of devotion. Duffy has usefully redressed a previous imbalance by depicting what he calls the experience of the conformist majority, people whose beliefs have often been ignored, misconstrued or disparaged in studies of the religious changes of the sixteenth century. But it is important to explore how much diversity of belief there was and how widely piety extended. These are difficult questions to answer, not least because replies are influenced by the norm against which they are measured. In comparison with England in the late twentieth century, early sixteenth-century society was undoubtedly very religious, with what appears to later generations a remarkably uniform set of beliefs. But this does not mean that there was universal adherence to those beliefs, nor that everyone believed with the same intensity or in the same way.

Any discussion of these issues needs to start by recognizing that the church was a very powerful institution, the owner of a quarter of the land in England. Much of this was held by religious orders: in a population of 3 million there were some 12,000 monks and nuns who had taken vows of poverty, chastity and obedience, dedicating themselves to the service of God within a religious community. The numbers of what we might call religious professionals were augmented by friars (whose orders owned little land since theirs was an itinerant calling) and by the many men in "holy orders". These included parish priests, priests employed to pray for the souls of the dead, and a host of other clergymen. Men with tonsures, a shaved patch on the top of their heads indicating their religious calling, were a very visible part of any community, a sign of the ubiquitous presence of the church.

The church exercised authority not only over those in orders but over the population at large. Everyone was subject to church law as well as to the laws of the state. There was an obligatory tax, tithe, lev-ied annually from all households on everything that was produced for the support of the church and the payment of its personnel. All citi-zens were required to attend their parish churches on Sundays and holy days. Like speed limits today, these laws were often not enforced, but offenders could be brought before church courts. Such courts had jurisdiction over many other matters that in later societies would be the concern of civil rather than ecclesiastical authorities. They were involved in the proving of wills. Since they were responsible for ensur-ing that oaths were honoured, they dealt with disputes relating to mar-riage and legitimacy, adjudicating many cases in which one party claimed to be contractually bound while the other denied that a legally binding commitment had taken place. Infringements of society's moral code, cases of slander and various forms of sexual impropriety were also brought before church courts, the branch of the legal system with which ordinary people were most likely to have contact.

Given its power, the church was bound to be the focus of resent-ment. Often this was directed against clergy who were the beneficiar-ies of tithe, and who had the right in the confessional to probe into the uncomfortable secrets of people's lives. The wealth and luxury enjoyed by some ecclesiastical dignitaries was an obvious source of complaint, as – common in all centuries – were sexual lapses among priests. But there is little evidence of much opposition to a clerical caste as such. Criticism by lay people, as by members of the clergy themselves, was directed primarily against clerical misdemeanours, against clergy who by their extortion, licence, or laziness failed to live up to people's ideal of what a priest should be.

The power of the church was buttressed by that of the community. There was far less privacy than there is today and decisions on what we would see as personal matters were in the public domain. Popular rituals involving public humiliation enabled communities to censure what they regarded as inappropriate behaviour. Men who allowed themselves to be cuckolded, wives who beat their husbands, women who contracted unpopular marriages were all subjected to noisy and embarrassing expressions of corporate disapproval. The church courts were not just – or even primarily – means whereby those in authority exercised control over those below. Ordinary people regu-larly used them to settle disputes such as slander among themselves. Adulterers were brought before the courts by their neighbours. To go against the moral values or dogma of a community was to threaten its very being, hence the silencing of persistent heretics.

The power exercised by both church and community militated in favour of conformity. This means that levels of nonconformity cannot easily be assessed, but court records reveal the existence of people deemed to be heretics. Often these were assumed to be followers of a fourteenth-century writer, John Wyclif, who combined anti-clericalism with the assertion that the Bible (not the church or the pope) was the sole source of Christian authority. Wyclifites became known as Lollards (from the Dutch word, *lollen*, to mumble) because they were keen Bible-readers and reading generally involved whispering words aloud to oneself. Fearful of being overheard they may have recited memorized passages to others in low voices. They were suspected because their Bible-reading led them to adopt views at odds with those officially propounded. Wyclif dismissed transubstantiation, the belief that bread and wine were changed into the body and blood of Christ, as an unbiblical novelty. The Bible seemed to imply that God had foreordained whom he was going to save: Lollards questioned whether there was any place for pilgrimages and prayers to saints which could be construed as actions designed to persuade God to change his mind. This challenge to accepted practices caused religious authorities to fear that if the Bible were freely available it would be misinterpreted. The involvement of some Lollards in an attempted coup in 1414 reinforced assumptions that religious unorthodoxy bred political subversion. Nevertheless, clusters of Lollards survived, particularly in the Chilterns, London, Essex and Kent, often passing on their beliefs through the generations.

Other men and women charged with unorthodoxy were sometimes labelled as Lollards although they had no connection with Lollard groups or teachings. Individuals who adhered to most of the church's teachings might, for example, deny the efficacy of directing prayer via the saints because their own prayers had not been answered. There were undoubtedly more instances of personal doubt of this sort than is recorded in the church records. The boundary between orthodoxy and heresy was not clear-cut.

So vast and unwieldy an institution as the church inevitably embraced some variety of opinion. Individual parishioners integrated inherited ideas, comments heard from priests and friars, and their own experience into an understanding of the faith which was both similar to and yet subtly different from that of someone elsewhere – or even someone in the same parish. Within the priesthood there was enormous variety, not least of educational standards. Some of the glosses provided by barely educated priests on the church's teaching caused their superiors disquiet. Although by twentieth-century standards the faith of our forebears may appear remarkably uniform this does not mean it was monolithic.

Variations in understanding can be well illustrated by popular superstitions. Keith Thomas cites the example of

> the communicant who did not swallow the bread, but carried it away from the church in his mouth . . . He could use it to cure the blind or the feverish; he could carry it around with him as a general protection against ill fortune, or he could beat it up into a powder and sprinkle it over his garden as a charm against caterpillars (Thomas 1971, Penguin edn: 38).

Living in a world over which human beings had little control, people understandably prized objects that seemed able to keep malign powers at bay or guarantee God's blessing. Mishap could be attributed to failure correctly to perform the associated rituals dictated by popular custom. Like us, our ancestors probably coped better with misfortune that appeared to be explicable than with that which seemed to be the product of arbitrary fate.

Thomas has suggested that popular belief of this sort was more superstitious than religious, more pagan than Christian. His interpretation has been questioned by Eamon Duffy, who challenges the assumption that popular superstitions can be starkly differentiated from the beliefs of the higher classes. If some commoners retained the communion bread in their mouths, some nobles built up their own private store of relics. That God offered himself in and worked through things material was a fundamental part of the church's creed. Priests taught that the world was molested by malign spirits, and that certain words, objects and gestures afforded protection against evil. The common people may have elaborated upon these beliefs in ways that invited condemnation by churchmen, but their ideas, far from being survivals of a pagan past, were not themselves fundamentally at odds with those propounded in church services. Thus Duffy suggests that there was less diversity of understanding between social classes, a more cohesive faith, than historians such as Thomas have assumed (Duffy 1992: 266–87).

During the quarter-century since Thomas wrote his book historians have increasingly stressed that religion and magic overlapped and that people drew on both resources. John Sommerville has pointed out that faith and folklore were often inextricably intertwined. Instinctively and without any sense of incompatibility people relied on a combination of prayer and what we might deem magic to tap superhuman resources: they recited spells, which included reference to the saints, to ensure the success of daily tasks such as churning butter. Sommerville warns against imposing the judgements of the present upon the past. Defining religion as that which gives access to the supernatural, he suggests that to treat such practices as authentically religious

> violates our tendency to side with the forces of progress. But we should be open to the possibility that superstition (a word we should avoid) is actually more religious than Christianity . . . "Superstition" may offer more avenues of access to the supernatural than a more refined faith (Sommerville 1992: 8).

Early modern society offered an enormous range of avenues to the supernatural with considerable variation in different parts of the country. Folklorists have identified customary practices peculiar to particular regions and there were also differences in popular devotion. Certain minor saints had a strong following in one part of the country and were unknown elsewhere. Veneration was offered not just to a particular saint but to a particular image, that saint in a particular place. Thus in popular thought Our Lady of Walsingham was different from Our Lady of somewhere else. People left money in their wills to specific images and roods, not just to the church in general. Belief in the holiness of objects and places was conducive to a localized faith.

The difference between localities was enhanced by institutional diversity. In some areas community life focused on the parish church, but in others parishes were far too large to be meaningful units of identity. Over the centuries additional chapels had been built to supplement parochial provision, known as chapels of ease since they facilitated access to worship. But in some parts of the country people identified more with a local monastery than a distant parish church or chapel of ease, and looked to the monks to meet their religious needs. Elsewhere profuseness of provision meant that neighbours might develop different religious loyalties: in towns there were often many churches, the ministry of roving friars and chantry priests, and numerous guilds and fraternities, each of which could provide a variant form of religious satisfaction. The religious complexion of one town might be very different from that of another depending on the influences to which it was exposed: access to trade routes, the varying approaches of the many different religious orders, and the customary practices of its hinterland. While people in the early sixteenth century used a common religious language, they spoke in different dialects, and rituals common to some would have seemed very strange to others.

Granted that piety took many different forms, the question remains: how pious was the population as a whole at the start of the sixteenth century? Churchwardens' accounts suggest that certain forms of devotion were widely practised. The vast quantities of wax sold for "lights" is proof that the custom of placing candles before statues to solicit saintly prayer was widespread. Many offerings were left by the populace at crucifixes, shrines and statues in ordinary churches as well as at major centres of pilgrimage. In 1524 the rood in Crediton Church, Devon, "was inundated not only by coins but also by coats of different colours, 93 rings, and a substantial collection of plate, girdles, buckles, pendants, brooches, crucifixes and beads" (Whiting 1989: 53). Personal possessions cited in wills and inventories provide further insight into popular faith. Testators well down the social scale regularly mentioned devotional artefacts that they wanted to pass on to family and friends: rosaries (strings of beads used in praying); medallions, small plates and pieces of cloth depicting the crucifixion; woodcuts of religious scenes; and above all rings bearing images of Christ, his mother, or one of the saints. The references suggest that such personal aids to devotion were both more common and more prized than is sometimes appreciated.

Other references in wills suggestive of piety are more difficult to interpret. Since it was universal practice to start a will by commending one's soul to God, the use of such pious formulae says nothing about the frame of mind of the people making wills. It can be argued that many who left money for Masses to be said for their souls were merely taking out last-minute insurance policies under pressure from priests who frequently acted as scribes. Testamentary evidence is thus no proof of piety in life. On the other hand, bequests made earlier in life would not be mentioned in wills; historians who use evidence of what people left at death as the main indicator of giving may underestimate levels of pious provision. While some testators were spurred into belated thought for the future by the proximity of death, bequests in the wills of others were part of an ongoing attempt to serve God and to ensure that they joined him in the bliss of heaven as soon after death as possible.

Some people treated the church's teaching with indifference or cynical amusement, prompting sermons criticizing their apparent disregard of the state of their souls. Threats of hell did not inspire everyone to godly living any more than threats of lung cancer today inspire everyone to give up smoking. There may have been a few men and women who doubted the existence of things supernatural. But even Susan Reynolds, who is concerned to stress the possibility of unbelief within the medieval world, takes pains to point out the prevalence of what she calls conventional piety (Reynolds 1991: 38–9). The religious culture of society and the ubiquitous presence of the church made it easy for those who were not deeply devout to seek access to the supernatural from time to time. As and when it seemed desirable, they participated in various forms of personal devotion – confession, Easter communion, lighting a candle before a saint – in real, if perhaps momentary, attempts to draw near to the divine. While for some those moments were rare, for others – maybe more than their secular-minded descendants imagine – they were a regular part of life.

It is impossible to tell what proportion of the population was conventionally and what proportion more deeply pious, and maybe it does not matter. What is likely to strike a twentieth-century observer is the dominant role that religion played within the life of society as a whole. Belief was expressed in a variety of different forms. Individual communities had their own devotional allegiances and customs. People interpreted the teachings of the church in more or less sophisticated ways, and internalized them to a greater or lesser degree. Some were cavalier about Christian observance and others, ranging from the sceptical to the deeply devout, articulated ideas that were regarded as beyond the bounds of orthodoxy. But the conviction that supernatural forces pervaded the world was commonplace. Religion was taken for granted as a natural part of life as people knew it.

CHAPTER TWO

The religious policies of Tudor governments, 1529–59

In the course of the sixteenth century, the religious culture of England underwent radical change. Until then there had been one universal or "Catholic", church in western Europe, headed by the pope in Rome. During the sixteenth century England, in common with some other territories, declared its independence of Rome; the English church was brought increasingly under state control and the king assumed its earthly headship. Monasteries, chantries and religious guilds were dissolved, and much of the wealth of the church was confiscated by the government. This included not only land owned by religious orders, but also objects from parish churches: bells, communion-ware made from precious metals, and richly decorated vestments worn by priests when celebrating Mass. The number of saints' days was drastically reduced; pilgrimages to shrines were forbidden and the veneration of relics condemned; statues and wall-paintings were defaced and roods were pulled down. Prayers and Masses for the dead, along with the use of palms and ashes, were banned, and Latin services were replaced by a vernacular liturgy. These changes constituted the English Reformation, part of a wider European movement.

The European context

In the early sixteenth century there was a groundswell of complaint about abuses within the church: moral shortcomings within the priesthood; the ignorance and sloth of some monastic communities; popular obsession with relics; the preoccupation with money epitomized in the sale of indulgences. Historians used to assume that these criticisms meant that the church was in a state of near terminal decline. More recent studies have stressed the vitality of pre-Reformation Catholicism, manifested in the building of churches and chantries, the continued formation of guilds, the popularity of pilgrimages, and the circulation of vernacular religious writings. New printing presses produced saints' lives, sermons, and lay guides to services. It was this enthusiasm about religion that prompted calls for abuses to be reformed. Critics came from within the church. They compared its present practice unfavourably with that of its first-century predecessor because they were anxious that it should fulfil its calling.

This comparison was facilitated by a new interest in classical learning and in the writings of the ancient and biblical worlds. Scholars became aware that over the centuries beliefs and practices had grown up that seemed to have no basis in scripture. Influential thinkers, such as Erasmus of Rotterdam, produced new editions of biblical texts, which challenged some traditional interpretations. The Greek word *metanoeite*, previously assumed to mean "do penance", was retranslated "change your mind", and this cast doubt on the whole idea of penance. A German monk, Martin Luther (1483–1546), protested that the church seemed to be teaching that people could earn or buy entry to heaven; he pointed out that this was contrary to the teachings of St Paul in the Bible.

It would be wrong to assume that these criticisms made the fracture of the western church inevitable. The church was in a state of constant evolution, hence the emergence in the medieval period of new feasts such as Corpus Christi and new beliefs such as purgatory. There had been reform movements before. While some had been suppressed, others had led to change and the development of new orthodoxies. But Pope Leo X (1513–21) neither heeded calls for reform nor acted decisively to silence them. When Luther posted his 95 theses criticizing indulgences on a church door in 1517, the pope saw no urgent need to deal with him; Luther appeared to be one more in a line of irritating young men whose wings the papacy had previously managed to clip. In any case it seemed impolitic for the pope to intervene in German affairs while an election for a new emperor, who would rule over German lands, was in progress. In the following three years Luther's views spread apace. This was largely due to the development of printing which was well advanced in Germany, a region rich in towns where new ideas were readily received and disseminated. By the time the pope and emperor sought to silence Luther in 1520–21, he had acquired much popular support. Papal condemnation made Luther a rallying-point for anti-clerical feeling and for the forces of German nationalism that objected to the interference of an Italian pope or Flemish emperor. Under the auspices of city fathers and the rulers of some German principalities, a Lutheran Church developed, its adherents subsequently dubbed Protestant, because they protested against the imposition of Catholic belief and practice.

The word Protestant was quickly applied to other new churches, which emerged as reformers and secular rulers elsewhere followed the example set in Germany. While there was considerable variety of belief among Protestants, they shared a common concern to do away with inessential accretions to the faith, which had accumulated over the centuries obscuring the central Christian message. They determined what was essential by reference to the Bible, which they saw as the primary source of Christian authority, revealing how the first Christians had understood and applied their faith. With the development of printing more and more people had access to the text. Many came to believe that the Bible taught that people were saved simply by trusting in Christ. There was no need for penance or any other compensatory payment to God because Christ had already paid all debts in full by dying on the cross. The demands of justice had been met – by God himself! Luther wrote

> 'Tis through thy love alone we gain
> The pardon of our sin;
> The strictest life is but in vain,
> Our works can nothing win . . .
> Wherefore my hope is in the Lord,
> My works I count but dust;
> I build not there, but on his word,
> And in his goodness trust.

Reformers expressed this theologically by saying that people were "justified" (or put right with God) "by faith through grace" (by trusting in the freely offered love of God) not by "works" (building up credit through saying prayers, giving to charity and going on pilgrimages). To people such as Luther who had long struggled to gain God's approval through prayer, penance and good works, the realization that all they had to do was gratefully accept what God offered was revelatory. It removed the strain of constant striving and prompted enormous gratitude:

> Though great our sins and sore our wounds
> And deep and dark our fall,
> His helping mercy hath no bounds,
> His love surpasseth all.

These beliefs led Protestants to develop other new emphases. The traditional teaching was that God's "grace", his loving acceptance of people, was conveyed through the offices of the church. Priests played a crucial role in this: you were forgiven the moment the priest pronounced absolution; failure to seek absolution meant that you would die unforgiven. Protestants argued that there was no need for priests to mediate between men or women and God. What was important was that individuals placed their trust in Christ, appropriating for themselves the forgiveness he was offering. Protestants proclaimed "the priesthood of all believers", maintaining that all who trusted in Christ had direct access to him and shared the responsibility of spreading the Christian message.

To those who adhered to orthodox teaching, Protestant ideas appeared very threatening. By questioning the role of priests and the church, Protestant reformers seemed to be overthrowing authority, destroying corporately held belief, and encouraging anarchy in which each person operated independently of others. They challenged people's deepest securities by denying that the living and the dead could help each other. The comfort of appealing to the saints and relying on the prayers of others was replaced by the stark insistence that each individual approach God alone. But the threat presented by Protestantism in the early sixteenth century should not be overstated. From the point of view of the authorities it constituted the most recent of a long series of heresies with which the church had always had to deal. The universal church, an integral part of society, had stood the test of time. That its unity might be destroyed and a multiplicity of new churches emerge was a barely conceivable idea. Few would have predicted that the break-away churches would be anything other than short-lived aberrations.

The English context

In England, as elsewhere, there were stirrings for reform in the early sixteenth century but it seemed unlikely that these would disrupt the established order. Reform was part of the ecclesiastical agenda promoted by energetic church leaders. The pope's representative, Cardinal Wolsey, closed down monasteries that were failing to attract new recruits. Among others, Bishop Sherburne of Chichester reorganized church courts under his jurisdiction, increased their efficiency, and regularly disciplined priests who did not do their parochial duties. More and more books were produced in English to help priests fulfil their pastoral responsibilities and to aid lay devotion. There was growing, if not widespread, interest in the new learning. Erasmus taught Greek at Cambridge from 1511 to 1514 and sympathizers such as Sir Thomas More propagated what became known as humanist ideas. These spread in the universities, in a few monasteries, in London and at court. All these people wanted to put their house in order, not to build anew. Men such as More sought to improve the church but had no sympathy with embryonic Protestantism.

Protestantism in England is sometimes traced back to Wyclif, who had challenged many traditional practices, although he did not teach justification by faith. Lollards may have paved the way for Protestantism in specific localities but their influence was necessarily limited. Those who refused to recant following conviction were still liable to be burnt at the stake. Luther's writings were known in England as early as 1519, but no widespread popular movement developed of the type that swept Germany. At the White Horse Inn in Cambridge, fellow members of Luther's order met with other interested readers to discuss his ideas, but those who propagated such views were subject to interrogation by the authorities; some sought refuge abroad. The king, Henry VIII (1509–47), was one of the most fervent Catholic monarchs in Europe, and in 1521 had been awarded the title "Defender of the Faith" by the pope for writing a book that denounced Lutheran teaching. The initials FD are still engraved on English coins as a memento of this. Since the success of the Reformation in any territory depended to a considerable extent upon the sanction of the ruler, England appeared to be one country that would remain safely within the Catholic fold.

Even highly orthodox kings had come to blows with the pope in the past. Most were determined to maintain their own authority and the autonomy of their nations against papal encroachments. Popes might exercise spiritual authority over kings, but they were often dependent on them as allies to protect territory that the papacy possessed in Italy. This gave rulers a lever to extort new powers over the church: kings in England, as elsewhere, had gained the right to nominate bishops (churchmen set in authority over the priests in a particular area or diocese), and had sometimes managed to negotiate a reduction in taxes due to the pope. The independent rights of the church were a constant source of irritation and gave rise to regular power battles between English religious and secular authorities. Civil lawyers tried to reduce the role of church courts. If churchmen trespassed on royal authority they were liable to be charged with a criminal offence, known as *praemunire*. Much of the national wealth was in ecclesiastical hands, and financially constrained governments were anxious to tap this. In the fifteenth century, parliament had called abortively for the state to take over church lands. Henry VII (1485–1509) kept bishoprics vacant so that their revenue could accrue to the crown, and new bishops had been required to pay a fee on assuming office. While these conflicts in themselves would not have prompted reformation, they contributed to a climate in which it was possible for a monarch to extend his authority over the church.

"The king's great matter"

The trigger for the Reformation in England was Henry VIII's battle with Rome over the validity of his marriage. A monarch's primary duty was to secure his dynasty. By the 1520s Henry and many of his advisers were deeply disturbed that he had not fathered a legitimate male heir. Accustomed to look for God's hand in all that did and did not happen, Henry could only assume that he must have offended God, who was withholding from him a blessing so essential for the future peace of the realm. He concluded that his marriage, dogged by miscarriages and still-births, was unacceptable in God's eyes. This interpretation was given additional force by the fact that Pope Julius II (1503–13) had been asked to give special permission for Henry to marry his brother Arthur's widow, since certain biblical verses forbad union with a brother's wife. Had Pope Clement VII (1523–34) been prepared to declare that the marriage was unlawful, the English Reformation would not have taken place in the way it did, if at all. But a pope who overruled a decision made by a predecessor undermined papal authority. In any case Clement dared not alienate Queen Katherine's powerful nephew, Charles, ruler of the dominant Habsburg empire, whose troops had recently sacked Rome. The pope's lack of responsiveness to the king's "great matter" meant that step by step Henry took the law into his own hands.

Henry did not plan a reformation. Annoyed that the church through its spokesman the pope would not do what he wanted, he hit out at the people close at hand, threatening the clergy with *praemunire*. The more they opposed him, the more the king asserted royal rights over those of the church. Anti-clerical lawyers had for some time been arguing in favour of secular supervision of the church as a way of curbing abuses, and a group of Henry's advisers produced a selection of ancient texts that seemed to confirm that England had always been a separate province of the church, answerable only to the king in religious matters. There was a wide range of views on these subjects both within the church and within parliament. Only after considerable debate did parliament agree that certain types of cases, including divorce, should be dealt with by English church courts, not Roman. This made it possible for the new Archbishop of Canterbury, Henry's nominee, to proclaim his marriage to Katherine void.

Kings had flouted the pope's will before and few would have predicted that this would lead to a lasting break with Rome. The deaths in 1536 of Katherine and of Henry's second wife, Anne Boleyn, made reconciliation feasible, but by then Henry and his advisers were convinced that the pope had exercised an illegitimate authority. This was reflected in the wording of the 1534 Act of Supremacy: the act did not *make* Henry head of the church in England but declared that he "justly and rightfully" *was* its head. The king was reclaiming what he saw as his rightful authority over the church in his domain.

The Henrician church

By taking charge of the church Henry did not make it Protestant. Indeed the confessional labels "Catholic" and "Protestant" are probably not helpful guides to opinion in the 1530s, for many people held what successors might see as an amalgam of views. Some of Henry's counsellors, such as Stephen Gardiner, Bishop of Winchester, and Edmund Bonner, future Bishop of London, continued to uphold Catholic doctrine while supporting royal supremacy. Some people hoped for the introduction of a vernacular Bible, sometimes seen as a Protestant innovation, but held to the traditional Catholic belief in transubstantiation. Among the innovative young clergymen who surrounded Anne Boleyn were men who were to become leading Protestants and others who never renounced their fundamental Catholicism. The direction in which they moved was in part determined by their reaction to Henrician developments.

By asserting authority over the church in England Henry made some measures of further reform inevitable. The onus for dealing with ecclesiastical shortcomings now rested with him, and those who had long demanded reform were eager for action. The king had considerable sympathy with those who sought to purge the church of abuses. While acknowledging that images could usefully serve as "books" for the unlearned, royal injunctions criticized the "offering of money, candles, or tapers to images or relics, or kissing or licking the same" (quoted, Gee & Hardy 1910: 277–8). This was seen as tantamount to idolatry, the worship of man-made artefacts, condemned in the Bible. Orders were issued for the removal of images to which offerings were made. Sharing his predecessors' vexation at the church's excessive share of the nation's wealth, Henry authorized a survey of ecclesiastical revenues, the *Valor Ecclesiasticus*, to pave the way for a redistribution of national assets. The substantial property of religious orders, abolished between 1536 and 1540, was appropriated to the crown.

With the wholesale dissolution of the monasteries England seemed to be moving in a more explicitly Protestant direction. At its best, monasticism had enabled dedicated people to draw closer to God by living a life of prayer and devotion. The phrase "the religious life" referred to life in a religious order, and this had long been extolled as the highest form of Christian service; people not in orders were regarded as second-class religious citizens. The incompatibility of this assumption with belief in the priesthood of all believers may explain Protestant antagonism to religious orders. In Protestant eyes the monastic life was yet another attempt to earn salvation by saying prayers. Religious orders were also suspected because they owed allegiance to organizations that transcended territorial boundaries and were therefore less amenable to the control of secular authorities than the population at large. Elsewhere in Europe the overthrow of papal power was invariably followed by the disappearance of religious orders. Members of these orders had been among the most vocal opponents of royal supremacy. It is not surprising that Henry's chief minister, Cromwell, a Protestant sympathizer and a man concerned to extend the state's power, sought to suppress them. Humanists had called for the selective closure of lax religious communities, and it is likely that Henry was inherently more sympathetic to this discriminating reform than to wholesale destruction. But he needed money to protect his realm against foreign attack. His anxiety to procure ready cash can be seen in his willingness to sell off monastic lands to anyone who could afford them, a move that lessened his immediate financial difficulties by alienating the capital that might have provided future income. Once the land had been sold there was no chance of reinstating the monasteries.

Henry's concern to raise money for national defence highlights the diplomatic considerations that made it desirable for England to move in a Protestant direction. By discarding Katherine he had antagonized the Catholic Habsburgs, the greatest power in Europe. If Charles V were to attack him Henry would need Protestant allies; at the same time the Protestant princes of Germany saw England as a useful associate should Charles seek to reinforce Catholicism in his German-speaking lands. Henry was not prepared to accept alliance at any price, and he refused a German demand that England adhere to a Lutheran confession of faith. Nevertheless, whenever the international climate looked threatening, he agreed to negotiations with the German princes. In 1540 he signalled his concord with them by taking as his fourth wife the sister-in-law of the Lutheran Elector of Saxony, Anne of Cleves.

While a number of interests and circumstances inclined Henry towards religious change, he retained many traditional beliefs. His annotations on draft statements of belief reveal that he never accepted justification by faith; he believed strongly in transubstantiation and he continued to adhere to the concept of purgatory. On the other hand he opposed the necessity of confession to a priest, and he defined the role of those in holy orders in decidedly Protestant terms, seeing them primarily as preachers and teachers of the Bible, not as men whose chief glory was to celebrate Mass. Unlike Protestants who pointed out that the Bible did not enjoin clerical celibacy, he continued to insist that priests should not marry. This amalgam of views is explained by a biographer who comments: "Henry . . . was never a Lutheran; indeed, in some matters he was intransigently conservative. But that febrile, wayward mechanism, Henry's mind, was in ferment – exploring, questioning, seizing on novelties, often pushing far away from its theological past, juxtaposing new and old in a curious medley" (Scarisbrick 1968: 399–400).

Henry's willingness to rethink his ideas can be seen in his changing attitude towards a vernacular Bible. One of the legacies of Lollardy was greater suspicion among English authorities of vernacular scriptures than existed in the rest of Europe. It was feared that these encouraged heresy. In 1409 possession of English translations of the Bible had been banned unless sanctioned by bishops. Whereas there were many French and German versions of parts of the Bible by the end of the fifteenth century, no printed text appeared in English until William Tyndale produced his New Testament in 1526, and this was printed in Germany. Henry disapproved of Tyndale's version, not least because the marginal notes of later editions were distinctly Lutheran in character. However, under the influence of Cromwell and Anne Boleyn, his antagonism to an English Bible was gradually overcome. Permission was given for a version by Miles Coverdale, free of offensive notes, to be published in England, and in 1539 a revised text by the same translator, the Great Bible, was given authoritative status. Parish clergy were urged to ensure that an English Bible was provided in every church.

Notwithstanding this legitimization of the vernacular scriptures, considerable doubt about their value remained. While some of the translators at work in the 1520s and 1530s knew Greek and Hebrew this was not true of all, and they drew heavily on each other's work. Coverdale's 1535 text was very dependent on translations into German and English by Luther and Tyndale respectively. Faced with a choice of possible English synonyms for a Greek term, Tyndale tended to favour those with a Protestant rather than a Catholic flavour. Thus, the translations themselves were sources of contention: while Protestant sympathizers objected that much Catholic teaching had no foundation in holy writ, those of Catholic inclination argued that translators were wilfully misrepresenting the text. There was anxiety that unschooled people let loose with the New Testament might mis-construe Christian teaching. Repudiating the Protestant claim that the Bible spoke for itself, Bishop Gardiner insisted that scripture had to be interpreted; the only way to safeguard against false interpretation was to leave the text in the hands of trusted expositors, the priests.

Henry's growing sympathy with these views derived from his fear that reform was acquiring an uncontrollable momentum of its own, conducive to disorder and anarchy. There was some justification for his concern. Some Protestant enthusiasts assumed that the king's orders to destroy images to which offerings had been made legitimized the destruction of any images. The dissolution of the monasteries was inevitably accompanied by looting and plunder. Henry was willing to give people access to the Bible but he did not want them to draw from it conclusions that did not correspond with his own. That could lead to diversity of creed and practice, regarded as highly dangerous in the early modern world. Pre-Reformation Lollards, each interpreting the Bible for themselves, had developed a range of religious beliefs, some decidedly bizarre. Once Henry had repudiated papal authority, new teachings from the Continent flooded into England, contributing to a ferment of ideas in cities such as London, from which those who had a taste for such matters might pick and choose. In his last speech to par-liament Henry complained that the "most precious jewel, the Word of God, is disputed, rhymed, sung and jangled in every ale-house and tavern" (quoted, Dickens 1989 edn: 213). Henry did not want dispu-tation, and he may well have been genuinely shocked by what seemed to him the cheapening of that which was holy. After Cromwell had fallen from favour following his unhappy attempt to yoke Henry with Anne of Cleves, Gardiner's more conservative views chimed in with the king's mood and inclinations. In 1543 an act of parliament restricted access to the English Bible.

In other areas of reform Henry tried to put a brake on changes that seemed to him to be getting out of hand. The six articles of religion, which laid down authorized religious belief in 1539, were noticeably more Catholic than the ten articles that had preceded them in 1536. Transubstantiation was affirmed and clerical marriage condemned. While Henry had been anxious to get rid of what he saw as super-stitious practices, it appears that what he really wanted was not full-blooded Protestantism but a reformed Catholicism, the old reli-gion, purged of its excesses, under his authority, not that of the pope.

There has been much debate about Henry's plans for the country after his death. His removal of Stephen Gardiner's name from the list of those who were to govern during the minority of his son has led some to wonder whether at the end of his life he was moving towards more Protestant views, a conclusion supported by his contact with reformist bedchamber officials. However, since Gardiner had caused Henry considerable irritation, his fall from favour may not point to any significant change in the king's religious outlook. Henry probably did not intend to enable a strongly Protestant faction to seize power after his death, but the discrediting of Gardiner and the Duke of Norfolk made this possible. Norfolk had fallen from favour by association with his niece, Henry's fifth wife. The position of counsellors of Protestant persuasion was further strengthened by the continued presence of Thomas Cranmer as Archbishop of Canterbury. Over the years Cranmer had gradually moved towards more Protestant convictions, and his survival was directly attributable to Henry, who had protected him against conservatives anxious to get rid of him. Henry retained a strong liking for and personal loyalty to the archbishop who had annulled his first marriage; this overrode their growing religious differences and even Cranmer's illicit marriage. Henry's last wife, Katherine Parr, supported reform, as did the tutors appointed for the royal children. When nine-year-old Edward, son of Henry's third wife, Jane Seymour, inherited the throne in 1547, he was surrounded by people who welcomed the opportunity of extending the Reformation.

The Edwardian Reformation

It was in the years after 1547 that the country moved in a decidedly Protestant direction. Whereas Henry had tried to curb what he saw as the misuse of images, Edward's council, after initial compromise, sought to remove images altogether. Protestants believed that prayer should be made directly to God, the sole source of human wellbeing, not through saintly intermediaries and certainly not through man-made representations of those intermediaries. Believing that admission to heaven was secured by Christ's merits alone, Protestants vehemently opposed prayers offered on behalf of the dead. The government confirmed orders for the dissolution of chantries, outlawed religious guilds, which existed to cater for needs after death, and transferred to the crown all endowments established to lessen benefactors' suffering in purgatory.

Most early Protestants believed that God communicated with human beings primarily through the Bible. This meant that they perceived truth as conceptual, and doubted claims that spiritual reality could be expressed and embodied in things material. They dismissed as superstitious the belief that certain objects had power in themselves to keep evil at bay. The consecration of candles at Candlemas as talismans against evil was banned, as was the sprinkling of congregations with holy water to bless and protect. Their emphasis upon the "Word of God" led Protestants to disparage rituals that communicated through senses other than hearing. Edward's council prohibited processions, the use of Ash Wednesday ashes and Palm Sunday palms, and the custom of "creeping to the cross" on Good Friday. In Protestant eyes these colourful and symbolic Catholic ceremonies were likely to obscure rather than illuminate God's purposes, providing the masses with the illusion of religious observance that was no substitute for meditation on the written word. In the past, statues, crucifixes and stained-glass windows had informed people about their faith. In Edward's reign orders were issued for their removal. All bans on reading the Bible were lifted, and English services were introduced. With the king's approval, Cranmer had spent the last years of Henry's reign writing English liturgies, and his authorized English prayer book was introduced in 1549, followed by a revised version in 1552. In the long term these writings were to do more than anything else to mould the character of the developing Church of England.

The Marian restoration

In the short term, the Edwardian reforms were soon rescinded. When Edward died prematurely in 1553, he was succeeded by his Catholic half-sister, Mary, the daughter of Katherine of Aragon. Mary reinstated Catholic ceremonies and liturgy, and commanded churches to reinvest in all the accoutrements of traditional worship. Clergy who had married under legislation passed in Edward's reign were brought before the courts and deprived of their livings. Clerical celibacy symbolized the difference between lay people and priests, who were privileged to handle the body and blood of Christ in the Mass; by disciplining married clergy Mary affirmed the distinctive character of holy orders. The country renewed its allegiance to Rome.

Even had she wanted to, Mary could not have brought about a complete restoration since some changes were irrevocable. In the 20 years since the dissolution, many erstwhile monks and nuns had died, others had married or been absorbed into new occupations; only a very small number approached the queen asking that they might return to monastic life. Moreover, few lay people, however devout, were prepared to give back monastic lands for which they had paid good money, particularly as no-one could guarantee that this set of changes would last any longer than those that had immediately preceded them. There was also doubt about the wisdom of re-establishing the religious guilds that had once played so dominant a role in lay life: those who had seen so many endowments confiscated could have no confidence that investments would be used for the purpose specified.

Mary did not aim to reintroduce everything her half-brother had abolished. Influenced by humanist teachers, she made no attempt to re-establish the great shrines and the cult of the saints with the accompanying veneration of their relics. Her own faith centred on the offering of Christ in the Mass, and it was this above all that she wished to reinstate. In restoring the Mass to England she believed she was giving her country the greatest possible boon, God present in his chosen form in the midst of his people. Each time Mass was celebrated the sacrifice which Christ had made that first Good Friday was offered anew; worshippers were enabled to gaze on his body and his blood given not just in time past but daily for their redemption. While Protestants' views on the "eucharist" or "communion" varied, there was widespread objection to the idea that the bread and wine were actually changed into the body and blood of Christ. The Latin words "*hoc est corpus meus*" – "this is my body" – were transposed in Edward's reign into "hocuspocus", signifying Protestant contempt for transubstantiation. Altars were replaced by common tables in order to remove any illusion that a sacrifice was being offered each time communion was celebrated. Christ's offering on the cross had been unique and unrepeatable, in the words of Cranmer's prayer book "a full, perfect and sufficient sacrifice . . . for the sins of the whole world". Any further sacrifice would detract from that which had already been made. In the eyes of many Protestants, Catholic teaching about the Mass epitomized the misconceptions under which that church laboured, the insistence that Christ's work was somehow not sufficient in itself. In the eyes of many Catholics, Protestant denial of transubstantiation was the ultimate heresy, for Protestants were closing their eyes to the very presence of God in their midst.

Mary put those who persisted in heresy to death, a course of action that earned her the epithet "bloody Mary". Her behaviour was not so unusual as this might suggest, for states had for centuries used the death penalty to secure uniformity of belief. Burnings were commonplace in Europe. Mary's father had committed extreme Protestants to the flames, while at the same time executing Catholics who refused to acknowledge his supremacy. The 1539 act of six articles had made death by burning the penalty for denying transubstantiation, and forbad judges to commute this to some lesser punishment. This measure was rescinded under Edward but a few Protestants whose beliefs seemed to exceed the bounds of orthodoxy were burnt in his reign. Mary's burnings were on a greater scale and took place in a more concentrated period of time than those which had preceded them but they were not out of tune with the ethos of the age.

Killing – and dying – for belief is something that those who live in more pluralist societies find hard to comprehend, whether in our own past or in other countries today. In order to understand it, we need to remember the horror in which heresy, however defined, was held. "There cannot be a greater work of cruelty against the commonwealth", commented Mary's adviser, Reginald Pole, "than to nourish or favour any such [heretics]. For be you assured, there is no kind of treason to be compared with theirs" (quoted, Brigden 1989: 606–7). The traditional fear that heresy would split a community apart was being realized only too obviously in sixteenth-century England which had suffered a series of rebellions in which religion played a part. Far from reflecting corporate identity, parish processions had become occasions of dissension: some Protestants jeered when the casketted host was paraded round the streets of London in Corpus Christi festivities. Protestant teaching had already led many astray and Mary feared that if it was not suppressed it would contaminate the spiritual and moral values of the whole community.

Burning was the last resort. Mary and her agents were primarily concerned to convert by persuasion. What Mary wanted was a populace that once again embraced Catholic orthodoxy. With a few influential exceptions – notably Thomas Cranmer, who had annulled her mother's marriage – those who recanted were spared the flames. The threat of burning was designed to enhance awareness of the heinousness of denying Catholic faith; the burning of heretics' bodies merely prefigured the burning of their souls in hell and might serve to warn others of the fate, temporal and eternal, which awaited them if they contradicted the teaching of the universal church.

The burnings did not achieve their ends. Admittedly at the start of Mary's reign there had been some concurrence in the attempt to root out Protestantism with neighbour reporting on neighbour. In some cases this may have been a way of settling old scores; the confidence, apparent self-righteousness and zeal of some radicals who had for years declared that they were right and the rest of the community wrong may well have been long-standing causes of irritation. Divided parishes may have seized the opportunity to get their own back on churchwardens who had enthusiastically pulled down images, removing treasured and familiar objects of devotion. But as the burnings got under way anger turned to sympathy for the victims. Heresy was recognized as a serious crime, but it is likely that its enormity in the popular mind was lessened by the fact that today's heresy was yesterday's orthodoxy: Protestants who adhered to the teachings of the second Edwardian prayer book were among those condemned. Inevitably people who had the courage to die for their beliefs inspired respect, and in Mary's reign there were nearly 300 of them. Their stories were told by that most skilful Protestant propagandist, John Foxe, whose popular book of martyrs moulded English perceptions of Catholicism for generations to come. "Be of good comfort, M. Ridley", Bishop Latimer reputedly exhorted his fellow victim; "we shall this day lyght such a candle by Gods grace in England, as (I trust) shall never be put out" (Foxe 1570 edn: 1937).

The Elizabethan settlement

Latimer's hopes began to be realized with the accession in 1558 of Mary's half-sister Elizabeth, the daughter of Anne Boleyn. Under Elizabeth the English church became identifiably Protestant. For the third time in little over a decade, parishes were sent instructions for a major reversal of religious practice. The commissioners appointed to ensure that liturgical instructions were obeyed and objects of Catholic devotion destroyed, included many zealous Protestants who had spent Mary's reign in exile on the Continent. These men were often more rigorous in their demands than the injunctions that they were supposedly implementing. But Elizabeth possessed a flexibility of mind that some of her subordinates lacked. She was well aware of the need for stability and, unlike her half-brother and sister, was anxious to effect religious arrangements that would command, if not majority support, certainly widespread acquiescence. Historians have disagreed over Elizabeth's own intentions and the extent to which she was constrained by parliaments. Whatever the cause, the religious settlement effected during the 1559 parliamentary session in her name promulgated a more mellow Protestantism than that encouraged by her brother. Some liturgical practices that Edward's council had condemned were permitted and this helped appease those of more conservative or Catholic inclinations. Whereas her father had styled himself "Supreme Head" of the church in England, Elizabeth adopted the title "Supreme Governor". This may have assuaged anxieties about female headship and was certainly less offensive to Catholics who affirmed the pope as head of the church, and to extreme Protestants who insisted that Christ alone was head.

The Elizabethan compromise is well illustrated in the communion liturgy of the 1559 prayer book. The 1552 injunction, "Take and eat this in remembrance that Christ died for thee, and feed on him in thy heart by faith with thanksgiving", seemed to imply that communion was essentially an act of grateful remembrance. It appears that Elizabeth herself believed that Christ was really present at each communion service (although not necessarily confined to the elements). At her instigation the 1552 words of administration were prefixed by those from the 1549 book, "The Body of our Lord Jesus Christ, which was given for thee, preserve thy body and soul unto everlasting life". This range of wording made it possible for people of varied beliefs to use the same liturgy. The 1559 prayer book was not so rigidly Protestant as to alienate people of Catholic sympathies.

Where Elizabeth could not and would not compromise was in her dealings with the pope, whose belief that she was illegitimate threatened her right to the throne. But in the 1560s as in the 1530s there was little public complaint about the break with Rome. In the early years of the Reformation people had objected to the destruction of images, shrines and monasteries, but it was Catholic practice most had sought to preserve, not Roman jurisdiction. Even J. J. Scarisbrick, an historian anxious to stress how deep-rooted England's Catholic loyalties were, comments "Papal authority in England ... did not matter very much in daily life" (Scarisbrick 1984: 60); "it was probably not often an object of personal commitment" (Scarisbrick 1968: 242). The pro-Catholic rebels of 1549 had marched through Cornwall and Devon objecting to the new prayer book and calling for the Latin Mass but they did not demand the reinstatement of papal supremacy.

Positive dislike of Rome had grown during Mary's reign, largely because of her unpopular marriage to the emperor's son, Philip of Spain. English people, whatever their faith, had no desire to be tied to the apron-strings of Spain, and under Mary this seemed to be an inevitable corollary of the return to Roman allegiance. Spanish involvement in plots against Elizabeth and the growing expectation of an invasion reinforced the sense that Catholicism meant foreign domination. Increasingly, propagandists associated Protestantism with patriotism. When the Spanish Armada fell to pieces in 1588, a commemorative medal proclaimed that God "blew with his wind and they were scattered". The deity was now assumed to be on the Protestants' side.

Elizabeth's longevity did more than anything else to stem the constant religious reversals that had characterized mid-sixteenth-century England. Despite ongoing criticism, the religious settlement authorized in 1559 remained intact. A Protestant Reformation had been effected by force of law. The next chapter explores how the people of England reacted to changes that their governments had introduced.

CHAPTER THREE

The impact of the Reformation

The middle third of the sixteenth century witnessed a legislative Reformation but this did not necessarily mean that the new faith was accepted at grass roots level. We need to ask: how far did people change their beliefs in response to governmental directives? Was the implementation of a new Protestant order made possible by the presence of latent support for reform in the country? Or did parishioners cling to the faith of their forebears? If so, for how long? And if they retained traditional sympathies, how did governments manage to impose an alien religious order on them? It used to be assumed that the Reformation was a change waiting to happen, welcomed by a population disillusioned with a corrupt Catholicism. A. G. Dickens' widely respected *The English Reformation*, first published in 1964, stressed the early growth of popular support for the new faith. More recently, historians such as J. J. Scarisbrick, Christopher Haigh and Eamon Duffy have proposed that government-imposed changes were accepted only slowly and reluctantly by a population still wedded to traditional ways. A lively and ongoing historical debate has focused on whether change was fast or slow, imposed from above or embraced from below, on when and even whether England became a Protestant country. Our understanding of the process of change has been enhanced by research on the impact of the Reformation in particular localities. These prompted the revisionist thesis in the first place, but they also modified it by revealing variations between and within regions, towns and even parishes. This chapter examines the different reactions to the Reformation. It considers why certain long-established religious practices disappeared quickly while others proved more persistent. Thus it seeks to illuminate the complex process of religious change at local level.

Early antagonisms

One of the early and obvious consequences of movements for reform in England was a growing amount of community conflict. Whereas religion had once helped reinforce communal solidarity, now it began to cause division. Antagonism between reformers and traditionalists at St Botolph's, Aldgate, in London was so intense that the mayor was called in to restore peace. Opposing preachers had provoked conflict in the capital as early as the 1530s. Some people who had already encountered reformed ideas responded with alacrity to Henry's injunctions for a limited amount of image-breaking, in some cases taking the law into their own hands, and destroying much more than the king had intended. A Henrician Bishop of Salisbury sought to reduce Catholic practices in his diocese in advance of the king's instructions, as did some of the men appointed by Archbishop Cranmer to parishes in Kent. The bitterness that built up over the years can be seen in the zest with which the radical vicar of Adisham near Canterbury was denounced for heresy within six weeks of Mary's accession. In the following months the parish was riven by a series of disputes with different factions erecting and dismantling the communion table, and engaging in physical assault on the vicar.

Such early battles occurred most commonly in the south-east and East Anglia, regions in which Protestantism made its initial impact. It spread more readily in areas accessible to the Continent, and in communities whose trading contacts provided openings for outside influence, than in regions more cut off from new ideas. Places where Lollardy had flourished tended to be particularly receptive. Another factor was the nature of the terrain since Protestantism, a faith that depended on the preaching of the word, was disseminated less easily in the wastelands of the north and west with their huge unwieldy parishes than in the more compact communities of the southern lowlands. On the other hand, parishes subject to strong manorial control could sometimes prove very resistant to religious infiltration from without; the more mobile, independent population in towns and in woodland and pasture regions was often more responsive to new ideas than neighbours in more tightly knit crop-producing parishes. As this suggests, no area was homogeneous. There were concentrations of Protestants in several Suffolk towns, in grazing and textile areas, and in manorially weak villages, but in other parts of the county Protestantism seems to have made no headway before the reign of Elizabeth. East Sussex was a Protestant stronghold, neighbouring West Sussex much more conservative. Lancashire and Yorkshire were decidedly Catholic but both contained groups of Protestants. Reformed convictions were caught through personal contact and this frequently cut across geographically induced trends. Young men who had encountered new ideas while studying at university and the London Inns of Court introduced them to their home towns in return. Commercial contact with an enthusiastic Protestant convert could result in the creation of a Protestant circle in one northern town, while a very similar neighbouring community remained untouched. One parish might be exposed to the new teaching because the right to appoint its priest had fallen into the hands of a land-owner of Protestant sympathies, while adjoining communities still had incumbents of more conservative inclination. Thus while Protestants were more likely to be found in some parts of the country than in others, religious conflict could erupt far away from obvious Protestant centres – even in 1549 in the school playground at Bodmin, deep in the supposedly conservative south-west.

The appeal of Protestantism

Conflict arose because some people were powerfully attracted by the new faith and wanted to pass it on to others. To understand the appeal of Protestantism we need to appreciate the excitement evoked by the publication of the Bible in English. In the past most people had encountered scripture only in portions dealt out to them within the context of the liturgy. Even Lollards had access only to parts of the Bible. Now increasingly they were able to handle complete Bibles, printed and bound in single volumes. The use of English enabled people to get behind the Latin words and interpretations provided by priests, and discover for themselves what the Bible was saying. Like Luther many converts came to believe with relief and exhilaration that God's love and forgiveness were freely offered and did not have to be earned.

This realization was not only liberating but could also create a pleasant sense of superiority: the truth was simple and self-evident, but priests, the recognized teachers of the church, had failed to perceive it, obscuring God's good news in unnecessary rites and disciplines. The "folyshnesse" of "an olde doctour whych greatlye lamented . . . that he myght no longar make invocacyon to sayntes, and thought hym selfe halfe lost for yt" was derided by an ex-friar who shared the common Protestant conviction that new light had dawned after long centuries of superstition (quoted, Dickens 1959: 142).

It was exhilarating to believe that God spoke through his word to anyone, to women as well as men, to ordinary people, however lowly their status. The enthusiasm and expectancy the new faith aroused is well communicated in a letter from the young Robert Plumpton to his mother. Recommending what appears to be Tyndale's preface to the New Testament he commented, "yf it will please you to read the introducement, ye shall see marvelous things hyd in it. And as for the understanding of it, dout not; for God wil give knowledge to whom he will give knowledg of the Scriptures, as soon to a shepperd as to a priest, yf he ask knowledg of God faithfully" (quoted, Dickens 1959: 133).

Fascination with the Bible acted as a strong incentive towards literacy, but the ability to read was not universal among those of reforming sympathies. Historians have increasingly recognized that memory and oral transmission of material played a major role in partially literate societies. Accounts of Lollard meetings imply that passages from the Bible were sometimes recited (rather than read) to the gathered company. Texts were passed on with much greater accuracy than we might expect. With the development of printing and the greater accessibility of Bibles the memorization of texts became less essential, but groups gathered in homes and round the Great Bible in churches so that the literate could read aloud to their fellows. William Maldon of Chelmsford recorded how "divers poor men . . . brought the New Testament of Jesus Christ, and on Sundays did sit reading in [the] lower end of the church, and many would flock about them to hear their reading" (quoted, Dickens 1989 edn: 213). While Maldon subsequently learnt to read, others such as John Harrydaunce, a London bricklayer, never mastered the art. Charged with unlicensed preaching in 1537, Harrydaunce announced that "he all these thirty years hath endeavoured himself to learn the Scripture, but he cannot write or read" (quoted, Brigden 1989: 274). Harrydaunce's method of preaching, stringing memorized texts together with his own interpolations, explains why there was so much anxiety about allowing unlettered people access to the Bible. Henry's decision in 1543 to restrict Bible reading to nobles, substantial merchants, gentlemen and gentlewomen would not have been necessary had people of these classes been the only readers. Many of those put to death in Mary's reign were artisans and agricultural labourers.

Protestantism predictably proved particularly appealing to people who were already personally serious about religion. While some priests and members of religious orders were slovenly in their duties, others had taken vows because they were deeply devout. Some of these found their religious yearnings more fully satisfied in Protestantism than in Catholicism. The largely clerical universities nurtured and disseminated new ideas that appealed to some humanists and others dissatisfied with the current state of the church. Prior to the Reformation few would have dreamt of deserting the Catholic church (at that time an inconceivable thought) but once this became a possibility some (not all) slipped easily into Protestant clothes. Reformed teaching probably also met the needs of people who had wavered on the borders between heresy and orthodoxy, men and women of varying levels in society who had their own personal doubts about reverencing images, praying to saints and the central Catholic belief of transubstantiation. In all these cases Protestantism provided answers to pre-existing religious questions and aspirations.

At the same time reformed ideas proved attractive to the young who had little personal experience of Catholicism. In comparison with the faith of their elders, Protestantism appeared novel, radical and lively. Open-air preaching generated wild excitement on the streets of London and elsewhere. Eager Protestant evangelists sought to pass on the faith they had discovered and jeered at what they saw as crude Catholic superstitions. This inflamed their opponents, and defenders of traditional ways became ever more vocal in response. Religious slanging matches attracted hordes of apprentices and others anxious to join in the fun. The many young men who flocked to London may have been alienated in any case because prospects of future advancement were not good. Relatively free from the constraints of their elders, they slipped readily into irreverent and anarchic behaviour. Anti-authoritarian sentiments were expressed by mocking priests, pent-up energy and frustration by smashing images. Some no doubt joined in simply for the sport but others were prepared to go to the stake for their new found faith. Many of the Marian martyrs were very young.

The appeal of Protestantism was enhanced by its strong corporate identity. Gathering together to read the Bible, fighting side by side to remove images and other relics of the past from local churches, sharing a common vision of a brave new world as yet unrecognized by others, Protestant groups established strong bonds even before some were forced underground by Mary. Of some 40 lay people known to be Protestants in Lancashire at the start of Mary's reign, all but three had close links with others. Subsequent persecution probably reinforced group loyalties and mutual interdependence.

We cannot know how many committed Protestants there were prior to Elizabeth's accession. There were almost certainly more underground congregations than those for which evidence survives. Some Protestants conformed outwardly to Marian requirements while maintaining mental reservations. Ralph Houlbrooke cites the case of parishioners of St Stephen, Walbrook, who attended Mass without honouring the elevated host: they "do use eyther to hange downe theyre heddes at sacrynge tyme of the masses or elles sytte in suche a place of the churches that theye cannot see the sacrynge" (quoted, Houlbrooke 1979: 232). Others, living in areas the queen found harder to control, may have continued to practise their faith unmolested. In some places – Colchester, Ipswich, Coventry and Leicester – groups of Protestants came out quickly into the open on Elizabeth's accession, destroying Catholic symbols in their churches. The martyrs and exiles were thus the tip of an iceberg. In their eyes to recant or conform would be to deny the life-changing truth which God had vouchsafed them, to turn their backs on the God who had personally touched them. Their willingness to suffer for their faith is clear evidence of the commitment that Protestantism inspired in some of its early adherents.

The attraction of the old ways

Most historians now agree that there had not been time before Mary's reign for the new ideas to become widely embedded in society. In some parts of the country, notably the north and the west, there had been relatively little Protestant infiltration. The battles that raged in London and other southern communities are proof that the new faith was far from dominant even in areas in which it had made most headway. Even when they were aware of new ideas, most people probably continued instinctively to adhere to traditional beliefs and practices. Some were sufficiently incensed by proposed changes actively or passively to obstruct them.

The first major dislocation of normality, the dissolution of the monasteries, was an act of sacrilege that sent shock waves through the land. However inadequate monastic communities might be, they occupied sacred places that had been set aside for God; here over the centuries godly men had been buried and in some cases the relics of saints preserved. To attack monasteries and shrines was behaviour so presumptuous that it invited the wrath of God. Henry and his officials appear to have been aware of the horror that their actions evoked; some shrines were dismantled at night to avoid protest, while the government seized on any instance of scandal, malpractice or fraud that could be used as proof that it was right to get rid of them. The surviving remains of monasteries show that some new owners ignored royal injunctions to destroy them. The purchaser of Rievaulx Abbey was probably loath to desecrate land beneath which his parents were buried.

Antagonism to the closure of monasteries was particularly marked in the north, where monastic communities were far more closely integrated with their neighbourhood than was the case in the southern counties. While socio-economic factors may well have played some part in the group of risings labelled the Pilgrimage of Grace, it is noteworthy that "the suppression of so many religiouse howses" was the first complaint articulated by the men who rose in York in 1536 (quoted, Sommerville 1992: 26). Their religious discontent helped to unite them.

Thirteen years later, west-country rebels objected to the introduction of services in English instead of Latin. It is hard for later generations to understand the horror felt over the use of the vernacular, but it is likely that a major element of unease was the sense that things holy and mysterious were being dragged into the gutter. People might not literally understand liturgical Latin but the use of a well-cadenced language with reverential associations helped evoke the majesty and otherness of God. To do away with Latin was to hinder access to God. In a society that believed that words were agents of power, to cease using sacred words was an act of monumental folly.

Assaults upon parish churches were further causes of distress for in the space of a few years most were changed almost beyond recognition. The central rood screen, which separated the people's part of the church from that in which priests performed the mystery of the Mass, was pulled down along with the eye-catching life-sized figures that surmounted it. Evocative doom paintings and wall-pictures were destroyed or covered by whitewash, baldly embellished with written texts of scripture and a royal coat-of-arms. The comforting figures of saints to whom parishioners had long prayed and all the decorative accoutrements of worship which had helped them sense the majesty of God were removed from their lives, disrupting the fabric of how things seemed always to have been. Parish heirlooms donated by their ancestors were commandeered by commissioners who seemed to have little sensitivity towards symbols of community stretching back through the centuries.

In some cases astute local families took church plate into safe-keeping before commissioners arrived to confiscate it. Others purchased liturgical objects themselves in the hope that they might one day restore them to their proper use. The caches of vestments, ornaments and images that came to light on Mary's accession are proof that some parishes had sought to circumvent rather than obey the Edwardian commissioners. But many things could not be recovered: court records reveal the reluctance of some people to relinquish the cloths and ornaments they had acquired, while some treasures had been requisitioned or sold further afield. Valuables accumulated through centuries of generous giving could not easily be replaced. Nevertheless the level of re-provision that took place in Mary's reign suggests a degree of popular enthusiasm: many churches were re-equipped beyond legal requirements. Some parishes, particularly but by no means exclusively in the north, restored the Latin Mass before they were instructed to do so. Looking back wistfully many years later, Roger Martyn of Long Melford in Suffolk described how his parish church had looked in its prime and outlined its Catholic rituals. He hoped that "when time serve" his heirs would restore the few mementos of past glories that he had managed to preserve from mid-century depredation (quoted, Haigh 1993: 2).

Authority and acquiescence

If some people in the parishes retained a real affection for the faith in which they had been reared, how did Henry, Edward and Elizabeth manage to implement such substantial changes? Churchwardens' accounts, recording expenditure in local churches, are an invaluable source in answering this question. Inevitably records are incomplete and most that survive come from the southern two-thirds of the country. These point to a high level of compliance not only with Mary's injunctions but also with those of other monarchs; there appears to have been widespread acquiescence in the importunate, costly and ever-changing demands of successive governments. Roods which had been removed in Edward's reign were reconstructed under Mary, often at considerable local expense, before being pulled down yet again and burnt on Elizabeth's orders. Numerous matter-of-fact entries reveal other instances of spending to replace or remove that which had only recently been dismantled or reinstated: at St Michael's, Lewes, two shillings and sixpence was paid in 1548 for the defacing of two windows, and six shillings and eight pence six years later for their repair and the supply of a crucifix. Predictably displacement was often speedier than reinstatement, the removal of the old more quickly effected than the purchase of the new; but the accounts confirm that governmental demands were on the whole met with remarkable dispatch. Within three years of Edward's accession all images had been removed from churches whose extant accounts have been studied by Ronald Hutton, and in most cases windows had been reglazed and walls whitewashed. Notwithstanding the expense, most of these parishes had managed to purchase English Bibles – admittedly under threat of fines – within six years of the order to do so; similarly they introduced the second Edwardian prayer book service within the time specified and acquired its Elizabethan successor within a year of publication (Haigh (ed.) 1987: ch. 6).

An obvious explanation of this compliance is that the price of resisting zealous commissioners was simply too high. Wearing down opposition, the men sent round by Edward and Elizabeth returned again and again to check that images and books had been destroyed, and to collect corrected inventories of church valuables. Churchwardens were required to give evidence on oath that they had obeyed the latest set of injunctions and faced public humiliation for non-co-operation.

If acquiescence in change was partly a product of fear or weariness, it is also attributable to the belief that those in authority had the right to dictate what their subordinates should do and believe. State intervention in matters of religion was not new but an accepted fact of life. Throughout the fifteenth century sovereigns had authorized certain religious views while labelling others criminal, imposing death sentences on impenitent nonconformists. Sixteenth-century people, like those in some authoritarian regimes today, probably accepted as normative what we might see as intolerable. Revisionist historians assume that while they obeyed, their attachment to the old ways means that people must have done so with reluctance, and there is some evidence in nostalgic writings to support this. But we have little access to what went on in the minds of people whose contexts of thought were very different from our own. Their response to change may have been fatalistic rather than critical or approbatory. A Suffolk parishioner, who signed his will two days after Elizabeth's accession, left 20 ounces of silver towards the purchase of a new cross for his local church "yf the lawes of the realme will permyth and suffer the same" (quoted, MacCulloch 1986: 182). Does this phlegmatic realism mask deep yearning for the glories of the past, or reflect an unemotional resignation to the new facts of life? We can never know.

The impact of iconoclasm

Whether people welcomed, regretted or simply acquiesced in government-sponsored iconoclasm, it had a profound effect on firmly established patterns of belief and practice. The dissolution of the monasteries did much to destroy the concept of sacred space, places in which God was particularly to be found. Once buildings had been pulled down or radically restructured for domestic use, the memory of their previous usage soon faded. This does not mean that previous convictions were superficially held, but deeply ingrained loyalties can be quickly eradicated if uprooted from the soil that nurtured them. In the sixteenth century holy places were desecrated without obvious divine recrimination and this did much to divest old ideas of their credibility. In many places legalized destruction unleashed popular vandalism as previously powerful authorities were shown to be vulnerable. Once the cordon of protection that had surrounded monastic buildings was removed, people who would never previously have profaned them joined in the plunder. By their very nature some Catholic concepts and practices could not survive the attack made upon them. In many respects Protestants were right to assume that if they destroyed the shrines and representations of saints they would put an end to prayer directed towards them. Since people had traditionally believed that power was communicated through holy objects, the destruction of the objects removed access to the power. The public burning of once-venerated images was a blatant statement of their impotence.

The destruction of images may have contributed towards the dramatic collapse of the huge industry of prayers for the dead, a crucial aspect of late medieval religion. This is one of the more difficult changes to explain. Lay fraternities, abolished in 1547, could have been reinstated, had people so wished, during Mary's reign. That this did not happen on any substantial scale cannot simply be explained by reference to fears of further financial sequestration. Had people been convinced that they were averting future pain they might have been willing to run financial risks. Their failure to make large-scale arrangements to secure the wellbeing of their souls suggests that belief in purgatory had been severely dented. Patrick Collinson provides what he calls a "tempting if not entirely convincing" explanation: Protestant claims that people were wasting money and energy in seeking to avert the pains of purgatory may have occasioned relief "like that experienced by the jogger who is told that his regular morning exercise is in fact bad for his health" (Collinson 1990: 256). Prayers for the dead depended on belief in a community which stretched back through time. This was weakened as mementos left by previous inhabitants were removed from churches and as the bede roll, which listed benefactors, ceased to be read. In a society that relied upon visual communication "out of sight" meant "out of mind". Once the ways of remembering the dead had been destroyed, awareness of a community that transcended death could not easily be re-created.

The passage of time

One of the ways in which historians have charted the transition from Catholic to Protestant is through analyzing affirmations of faith and bequests in wills. These have to be used cautiously but they provide some impression of the extent to which Protestantism was advancing or Catholicism retaining its hold in different parts of the country. But some mid-century wills seem to combine both Catholic and Protestant affirmations: the testators stressed that they hoped to be saved only through the death and resurrection of Christ, but at the same time they asked for the prayers of saints. Were these statements perhaps made by people who had been sufficiently exposed to Protestant ideas to pick up concepts of Christ as sole redeemer, but who combined this with ideas of the intercession of saints from their Catholic past? It is possible that in the confused climate of the mid-sixteenth century they held an eclectic faith gleaned from both sources.

This sort of synthesis of belief could easily survive in the new Elizabethan liturgical climate. The 1559 prayer book contained much that was familiar from the past, particularly by way of ceremonial action. Clergy were instructed to put on vestments for preaching and celebrating communion; communicants were still expected to kneel; babies were signed with the cross in baptism, and a ring was given in marriage. The continuation of old practices facilitated the continuation of old beliefs. Theologians might stress that baptism signalled the reception of children into the church but it was still commonly assumed that the mark of the cross safeguarded them from harm; the marital ring was believed to give the wearer protection against unkindness and discord. The doctrine laid down in articles of faith might be distinctively Protestant but the meaning people read into what they heard did not necessarily correspond with what the writers intended. The fact that prayer book services took place in churches originally designed for Catholic ritual may have helped preserve some of the old rhythms of worship and made more difficult the introduction of more extreme Protestant practices.

In the early years of Elizabeth's reign the vast majority of services were conducted by conservatively minded clergy appointed under Mary and her father; only a few hundred priests left their livings when she reinstated Protestantism. The education of the clergy in reformed ways was a long-term task and it seems probable that many continued, with some adjustments, to do as they always had done. While they were no longer required to hear annual confessions nor permitted to say Mass for people's souls, they were still responsible for the spiritual welfare of all in their parishes, providing rites of passage and a regular round of services. Without necessarily intending to infringe injunctions, some would doubtless conduct prayer book communion services in much the same way as they had once celebrated Mass. When no "foreigners" were around, they might incorporate Latin prayers into the liturgy – and were occasionally caught out. Some observed forbidden feasts. Far more priests presumably continued to use holy water, indicted vestments and rosary beads than are recorded in official visitors' reports.

Elizabeth largely depended on local officials to monitor continuing obedience to the new laws. Justices of the Peace (JPs) such as those in Elizabethan Sussex who were sympathetic to the old ways were unlikely to seek out or deal severely with religious dissidents. Bishops attempted to impose order but those in charge of large dioceses with poor communications could not easily exercise authority; they might send visitors to check up on parishes, but communities sometimes closed ranks against inspectors from outside, refusing to report those who offended against the new regulations. It is, as David Palliser notes, a "depressing possibility that the records indicate only the distribution of small minorities of dissenters and that areas of widespread dissent might often pass unrecorded" (Heal & O'Day (eds) 1977: 53). The revisionists are surely right to stress continued support for traditional practices in early Elizabethan England. Parts of the North of England seem to have been particularly wedded to the old ways: when Edmund Grindal was appointed Archbishop of York in 1570 he was appalled to discover how many churches in his province retained roods and other items of Catholic worship.

In time these vestiges of the past were removed. Revisionists acknowledge that by the middle of Elizabeth's reign the religious climate was changing. Initially Cranmer's communion service may have been regarded as another form of Mass but in time the old associations disappeared. As clergy sympathetic to traditional rites died, they were increasingly replaced by men who had been trained at Protestant universities and knew only the new faith. Congregations which had continued some conservative practices gradually, maybe almost without noticing it, absorbed new ways. Reluctance to accept modified forms of worship merged into acquiescence and then into familiarity. And all the time new generations were growing up who could not remember the Latin Mass, and for whom older people's liking for rosary beads and holy water was a mere foible of age. Any traditional practice, however deeply rooted in popular affection, is likely to die out within a generation unless there are means of integrating it into the lifestyle of those who come after, hence the disappearance in the course of Elizabeth's reign of many of the old ways.

Spreading the word

The erosion of the old faith did not necessarily imply acceptance of the new. Protestant churchmen were well aware of the need to disseminate reformed beliefs to a people largely ignorant of them. Songs, woodcuts and engravings, caricature and drama were all employed to debunk Catholicism and to spread Protestant ideas to a semi-literate population. While some of the more ardent Protestants were later to object to dramatic presentations, in the early days Catholic mystery plays were counterbalanced by no less bawdy productions designed to inculcate Protestant beliefs and ideas.

The main means reformers used to spread their faith was preaching. Since Protestantism was a religion of the book, proclamation of God's word was perceived as all-important. In a society in which some people could not read, oral communication possessed a power it has since lost, and there was reason to believe that the pulpit was an effective agent of change. Some individuals attributed their conversion to Protestantism to the influence of a particular preacher, and the presence of charismatic clergymen was often a key factor in moving certain parishes in a Protestant direction.

But the Elizabethan church faced a major problem in that few of its inherited clergy possessed the ability to preach. Realistically the 1559 royal injunctions required that only four sermons a year be preached in each parish church (although, confusingly, they also insisted on monthly sermons!). Bishops issued preaching licences to clergy they deemed to be competent, generally graduates. Those who were not licensed to preach were expected to invite visiting preachers to ensure that their congregations heard some sermons, but it is clear that the minimal annual requirements were often not met. When no preacher was available, authorized homilies were to be read instead. These made some attempt to inculcate Protestant beliefs into a people brought up in Catholic ways, but many were essentially exhortations to socially responsible behaviour.

Elizabethan bishops made strenuous efforts to create a ministry more capable of instructing and persuading the populace. Over time the number of graduate ministers substantially increased. The sixteenth-century equivalent of in-service training was provided for ministers who did not as yet hold preaching licences: the 1559 injunctions required non-graduate clergy to engage in regular study, and dioceses made arrangements to monitor their progress, sometimes appointing educated ministers to act as academic supervisors to their less qualified brethren. In the 1560s and 1570s a corporate form of clerical training known as "prophesyings" became common. These were public meetings at which several sermons on one text were delivered; afterwards the ministers present met for instruction and discussion. The queen's intense suspicion of what she saw as radical religious gatherings and her dislike of preaching led to their suppression, but other opportunities for ministers and lay people to attend sermons continued to proliferate.

From the time of Henry VIII some Protestant activists had gone on preaching tours, travelling round to different towns and villages to preach the word, a pattern of behaviour mirroring that of Catholic friars. During Elizabeth's reign, affluent patrons provided sponsorship for such activity. Borough corporations and some individual benefactors funded lectureships. These frequently developed in place of indicted "prophesyings" and made possible the delivery of extra sermons ("lectures") on Sunday afternoons or weekdays. Sometimes a single individual was appointed to a lectureship; in other instances the endowment was used for a series of sermons by a local incumbent, or by a group of local clergy. While there were some variations in organization, lectureships became a common feature of market towns throughout the land, the support for them a clear indication that preaching had popular appeal.

In addition to preaching, clergy were expected to "catechize" their flocks. Catechisms, aphoristic question-and-answer instruction books, were designed to provide easily memorable synopses of Christian faith, appropriate for a semi-literate society. Often ministers published variants of their own which might more effectively meet the needs of congregations they were teaching. Ian Green estimates that there were some three-quarters of a million copies of these alternative catechisms in circulation by the early seventeenth century, as well as half a million of the official versions (Green 1986:

425). Many went through several editions. The sheer numbers published to cater for a population of 4 million suggests that catechizing was a major activity in Elizabethan England.

The Protestant emphasis upon preaching and teaching meant that over time clerical self-perceptions changed. Increasingly, clergy described themselves in their wills as "ministers of the word". A 1603 survey revealed that there were 4,830 preachers in the 9,244 English parishes, a substantial increase in the course of Elizabeth's reign. While there was still some way to go, attempts to create an educated ministry were clearly succeeding.

The religion of the people

It remains to consider how far these efforts had an effect upon popular belief and practice. To some extent this depended on where people lived. Catholicism persisted in Lancashire long after it had been eroded elsewhere. Protestant clergy worked in parishes and, through lectureships, in market towns. The parish system operated far more effectively in the central and southern lowlands than in the north. Here the spiritual needs of the population had previously been met as much through monasteries and chantry chapels, now defunct, as through the mechanism of vast sprawling parishes. People could more easily gather for "common prayer" in urban areas and compact rural communities than in regions in which a dispersed population lived miles from the nearest church.

As in the past, everyone was required to attend church on Sundays and feast days, but, as in the past, not everyone did. Absence was punishable by a fine of one shilling, levied by churchwardens, who were expected periodically to provide the church authorities with lists of truants. Those cited were liable to be called before church courts, as were the wardens themselves if they were deemed not to be fulfilling their supervisory duties. These arrangements suggest that persistent absentees were more likely to be presented than those who sometimes went to church and sometimes did not. There were clearly far more absentees than those who were reported. Absenteeism may have been particularly marked in the early years of Elizabeth's reign. As the century progressed, greater efforts were made to enforce attendance than had been attempted before the

Reformation, with the result that church-going may have increased in the 50 years following 1570. By twentieth-century standards a large proportion of the population attended services, if not every week, at least from time to time. Peter Clark, who stresses the amount of irreligion, has estimated that 20 per cent of the inhabitants of late sixteenth-century Kent were regular absentees, but this implies that four-fifths of Kentish people may have had some sort of contact with the church (Clark 1977: 156–7).

In addition to attending services on Sundays and holy days early Elizabethans were expected to receive communion three times a year. This requirement was quietly dropped in 1571, presumably because parishes did not co-operate, and the courts thereafter dealt only with those who missed Easter communion. The practice of communicating at Easter, inherited from the Catholic past, appears to have remained common. After 1559 lay people received both bread and wine rather than just the bread. The prodigious quantities of wine purchased point to large-scale attendance. The churchwardens' accounts of St Saviour's, Southwark, record that 67 gallons were bought between 30 March and 5 July 1594 to enable parishioners to attend a communion service in the weeks around Easter. A census authorized by bishops in 1603 indicates that only 1.3 per cent of the eligible population in London failed to receive communion. In Ely, another diocese for which there are clear returns, 2 per cent did not communicate. These figures are probably not typical of the country as a whole, but it is noteworthy that in popular parlance communion continued to be described as receiving one's rights. This suggests that people both expected and wanted to receive Easter communion and did not attend just because they were required to do so.

We do not know exactly who the absentees were. Some historians, such as Peter Clark, have assumed in the absence of definitive evidence that those who did not attend church were mainly members of the poorer classes. This is challenged by the figures from Southwark: St Saviour's was a poor part of London with a rapidly changing population, but over 87 per cent of parishioners eligible to communicate did so in 1603. An alternative suggestion put forward by Patrick Collinson is that absence was more a product of age than class, but there is little firm data to support this view either. We have no clear evidence whether children under 14 were expected to go to church. Once they reached this age they were required to attend services, and those over 16 were expected to communicate once a year. Adolescents and young adults were frequently the target of Elizabethan clerical complaints. This gives credence to the claim that this huge sector of the population was the group most likely to be estranged from formal religious observance (Collinson 1982: 224–30). As they took on adult responsibilities, which included financial contributions to the church, people may have become more integrated into the life of parish communities and more ready to share in communal worship.

The religious settlement of 1559 required parishioners to demonstrate basic religious knowledge before they were admitted to communion. Catechism classes, designed to provide the necessary instruction, were the clergy's main means of contact with the young. It is impossible to tell how far classes were attended but Ian Green points out that at the end of the century clergy were criticized less for failing to hold them than for conducting them with insufficient skill (Green 1986: 416). Clerical comments suggest that, as a result of catechizing, many children and adults became familiar with basic Christian doctrines. But ministers were uneasy about the way people construed what they were taught. A clergyman who lived in Kent reported that despite regular catechizing most of his parishioners believed "that a man might be saved by his own weldoing" (quoted, Collinson 1982: 202). Protestant instruction was not able to remove the traditional assumption that access to heaven could be gained by "good works".

Some preachers concluded that the bulk of the population were untouched by the reformers' message. The new faith had been introduced early into Essex, but in 1582 George Gifford of Maldon complained that the majority of people "having Popery taken from them, and not taught thoroughly and sufficiently in the Gospell, doe stand as men indifferent, so that they may quietlie injoy the worlde, they care not what religion come . . ." (quoted, Wallace 1978: 29). In view of such statements some historians have deduced that the Reformation encouraged the growth of religious indifference. But this assessment places too much reliance on the views of zealous Protestant activists. Ministers such as Gifford who complained of popular apathy were looking for precise theological understanding and personal spirituality. It was hardly likely that the conventionally pious would internalize the new faith to a far greater extent than they had the old.

For many people religion was essentially a matter of sharing in communal ritual, an approach to faith of which Gifford was contemptuous. He dismissed mere attendance at services as outward show, lip-service, popery and even atheism, but this is more revealing of the expectations of the critic than the religious state of the criticized. He may have failed to recognize some piety that did exist because it focused upon church attendance and thus took a different form from his own. Martin Ingram concludes that the faith of the majority was probably somewhere between the personal spirituality that men such as Gifford expected and indifference, a "stolid conformity which stopped well short of enthusiasm" (Ingram 1987: 94, 116).

While they may not have embraced reformed teaching in the way that some of its exponents wanted, it seems that English adults attended church in sufficient numbers and with sufficient frequency for the language of the Church of England to become a familiar part of their lives. In consequence they acquired, maybe subliminally, a supply of religious ideas somewhat different in emphasis from those of their ancestors. Patrick Collinson has suggested that the homilies and liturgy possessed "the capacity to distil and drop into the mind, almost by an osmotic process, familiar forms of words which may have done more than anything else to form a Protestant consciousness" (Collinson 1984: 179). This consciousness manifested itself in different ways. In some it was inextricably associated with the practice of parochial religion, attendance from time to time with others of their neighbourhood at their parish church. Some came to feel real affection for the Book of Common Prayer, the familiar rites of which were increasingly all they could remember. Others looked for something more, affirming that Protestant faith was less a matter of ritual observance than of inner devotion. The Church of England, like any church, was in a state of evolution and, because of the circumstances of its evolution, came to embrace a wide variety of beliefs. This diversity, one of the lasting consequences of the Reformation in England, will be explored in the next chapter.

CHAPTER FOUR

Varieties of belief

In the early sixteenth century there were no precedents for creating new churches. Protestantism, as its name implies, developed in reaction to what had gone before. Reformers were determined to get rid of inessential accretions to the faith, but disagreed about what these were. Some Protestants maintained that only abuses need be purged and that other Catholic customs could continue. Others insisted that anything not specifically affirmed in the Bible should be jettisoned. All appealed to the authority of the scriptures but interpreted them in different ways. New groups emerged as people developed new insights into aspects of the Bible, which they believed others had neglected at their peril. Just as today there are different schools of psychoanalytic thought, sharing common origins but deeply antagonistic to each other, so in the sixteenth century various brands of Protestantism developed differing in what they retained from the past and how they interpreted the Bible.

The theology of the English church

In the early years of the Reformation, when everything was still in the melting-pot, there was much excited interchange of people and ideas between different countries. The first European Protestants with whom the English had contact were German Lutherans, but in the longer term Luther had less influence in England than other continental Protestants. Among the refugees invited to England during Edward's reign was Martin Bucer from Strasburg, who gave Cranmer much advice on the content of the 1552 prayer book. With Mary's accession, those who had been hosts to persecuted Protestants went into exile themselves. German Lutheran states did not readily offer sanctuary to non-Lutherans, least of all those fleeing the emperor's daughter-in-law. English exiles gravitated instead towards non-Lutheran Protestant cities, particularly those in Switzerland.

The leading figure of the Swiss Reformation was John Calvin (1509–64), whose understanding of Christian doctrine was systematically expounded in his monumental *Institutes of the Christian religion* (1536–59). Calvin's reading of the Bible led him to assert that God was absolutely sovereign: in the Hebrew Bible (the Old Testament) everything was attributed to his will and direct intervention; in the New Testament Jesus taught that even the death of a sparrow was within the purview of a caring Father. This image of God as all-powerful and all-knowing lay at the heart of Calvin's theology. Calvin shared the common Protestant conviction that human beings were utterly sinful, in theological terms totally depraved. Unable to save themselves by their own efforts, they depended on the freely-given grace of God. The fact that only a limited number appeared to respond to God's love had to be explained in a way compatible with divine sovereignty. Calvin proposed that God had himself already determined who were to be redeemed. These people, the "elect", were "predestined" to salvation; they would irresistibly respond to God's grace and persevere in his service come what may.

Some of Calvin's followers took this idea further, giving it more emphasis than Calvin had himself. Men such as Theodore Beza argued that if some people did not respond to God's grace, that must be because God never intended them to accept it. It followed that Christ had died, not for all, but only for those who were predestined for salvation. Beza's theory of "double predestination" implied that the rest were doomed to damnation.

To modern minds these may appear singularly unattractive beliefs. But Calvinist theology was supremely coherent: everything Calvin and Beza taught followed logically from their initial premise about divine sovereignty. People fascinated by religious ideas struggled with complex questions that have troubled thinkers in all ages. Calvin provided a comprehensible explanation for otherwise unanswerable problems: everything that happened, good or ill, was determined by God. People today do not readily accept "God has decreed it" as an adequate explanation when things go wrong. But this response may have seemed less unacceptable in a society in which individuals had limited freedom to shape their own destiny. Calvinism was a theological expression of the apparently self-evident truth that life was arbitrary.

Calvin's ideas began to be disseminated in England within 15 years of the break with Rome. Edward VI and his advisers corresponded with him, and in Mary's reign a sizeable community of English exiles met him and witnessed his attempt to form an ideal Christian society in Geneva. During their stay they produced the "Geneva Bible", an English translation that contained marginal notes of a Calvinist nature. Sometimes dubbed the "Breeches Bible" (it suggests that Adam and Eve made themselves breeches from fig leaves), this was to become extremely popular in Elizabethan England. Those who could afford to go into exile frequently returned home to positions of influence. Given the shortage of candidates, Elizabeth had no option but to appoint 17 returned exiles to bishoprics. With few exceptions senior churchmen and university theologians accepted Calvin's predestinarian concepts as a way of understanding divine sovereignty.

These ideas probably did not impinge much upon the majority of people. Catechisms, which were drawn up in such astounding numbers in the course of Elizabeth's reign, tended to ignore potentially controversial topics such as predestination, concentrating on what the authors saw as basic Christian teaching: the traditional creeds of the church, the ten commandments, the Lord's Prayer and the meaning of baptism and communion. On the other hand predestination was an important part of personal belief for some Puritans, whose views will be discussed later in this chapter. In 1598 an ironmonger of Sleaford in Lincolnshire was among those who criticized a minister for speaking "somewhat disdainfullie of God's predestination" (quoted, Collinson 1989: 205). As the Church of England continued to evolve, such disagreements over Calvinism were to become more and more important.

Authority and structure

In Elizabeth's reign theology was less a cause of contention than church organization and the exercise of authority. The circumstances of its creation meant that the Church of England had inherited institutional structures from the Catholic past. Successive monarchs saw no need to alter a well-established and reasonably effective machine. Since England had constituted two provinces within the Catholic church, two archbishops continued to preside in Canterbury and York. Within each province bishops exercised authority over their various dioceses as they had before. Part of their responsibility was to examine would-be clerics who wanted to work in their dioceses, and ordain them as clergymen if they seemed suitable. But the right to choose who would be appointed to each parish lay elsewhere. Universities, cathedrals, the crown, officials, heads of powerful families and above all religious orders had traditionally possessed the right of presenting priests to particular parishes. With the sale of church property, monastic rights of presentation frequently passed into the hands of new lay land-owners, who now exercised much more influence over the church than they had before. But apart from this, the rationalization of some parishes, and the creation of six new dioceses by Henry VIII, the basic institutional structure remained intact.

Protestants who fled abroad under Mary encountered different systems of church organization. Isolated from English ecclesiastical controls, some exiles in Frankfurt seized the opportunity to create a self-governing, independent church. They developed their own liturgy from which all vestiges of Catholic belief and practice had been expunged. This brought them into conflict with fellow exiles, adherents of the 1552 prayer book, who were anxious to "do as they had done in England, and . . . have the face of an English church" (quoted, MacCulloch 1990: 83). Disputes of this kind continued on a larger scale when they returned to England.

Debates about church order may seem inconsequential to us, but to people at the time much was at stake. A major aim of the sixteenth-century reforming movements was to get back to the model of New Testament Christianity. Eager converts scoured the Bible to determine what form of church organization it authorized. But not all Protestants agreed that guidelines about such matters could be found in the scriptures. Some, including bishops who had once been exiles, maintained that on many issues, "matters indifferent", the Bible gave no clear guidance. In these cases the responsibility for laying down rules belonged to the statutory authorities. In contrast, radicals maintained that nothing was indifferent in the sight of God. The Bible might not give detailed instructions but the spirit of its general injunctions could be applied to any area of life. To ignore divine guidelines was to invite the wrath of God on a rebellious people.

These disagreements came to a head in a bitter dispute about what Church of England clergymen should wear, the vestiarian controversy of the mid-1560s. Clerical attire, inherited from the Catholic past, evoked powerful emotions among those who had watched friends and neighbours burned at the behest of those who wore such dress. Vestments symbolized the separation of priests from laity and this offended against the belief that a truly reformed church should have no priestly caste. By insisting that certain garments continued to be used, the queen seemed to be backing erstwhile Catholic clerics and denying the Protestantism for which the martyrs had given their lives.

It is possible that Elizabeth used clerical dress to exert control over her more radical clergy. Ministers who refused to wear the correct vestments tended to make their own decisions about other matters, ignoring instructions laid down in the Book of Common Prayer. In the sixteenth century diversity implied the collapse of an ordered society, a state of affairs that foreign enemies might all too easily turn to their advantage. Riotous protests by London mobs opposed to vestments reinforced fears that religious radicalism led to disorder. Bishops who were obliged to maintain order but had little liking for vestments were in an unenviable situation. Believing that what clergy wore was a "matter indifferent", which the statutory authorities had a right to determine, they imposed limited norms of clerical dress. This was regarded by protestors not as a necessary compromise in the face of royal pressure but as pusillanimous adherence to practices that could not be biblically defended. In the eyes of their critics the church's leaders were turning their backs on the Reformation.

This dissatisfaction with bishops reinforced demands for a fundamental restructuring of the English church. One of the hallmarks of a true church on the Genevan model was the effective exercise of discipline. Radicals believed that English bishops were failing to discipline incompetent clergy but were inappropriately impeding the ministry of those who sought to dispense with unscriptural practices. They argued that power should be exercised not by bishops appointed by the crown but by local and national assemblies to which congregations would send elected representatives. The assemblies in consultation with congregations should be responsible for appointing ministers to particular parishes and for disciplining those who failed to live up to their calling. Bishops should not be seen as a superior order of churchmen, since all ministers or "presbyters" were believed to be of equal standing, hence the labelling of this system of church organization "Presbyterianism".

From about 1570 would-be Presbyterians pressed their case vociferously in pamphlets and more circumspectly in parliamentary debate. In the 1580s sympathetic ministers gathered in voluntary local assemblies and held clandestine national gatherings. This apparent formation of a church within the church reinforced the suspicions of the authorities who feared that Presbyterianism could prove dangerously subversive. In 1591 various leaders were brought before the courts, and the Presbyterian movement was effectively quashed. The institutional structure inherited from the past continued to operate.

Underlying all these disputes was a difference of opinion about the status of the 1559 settlement. Some who had been exposed to what they saw as exciting developments on the Continent suffered intense frustration at the caution and conservatism of Elizabeth's regime. There was disappointment at what appeared to be the tardiness of bishops in introducing further reform. Many keen Protestants saw the 1559 arrangements as an interim measure, a step on the way to a more fully reformed church. They were horrified to discover that the queen regarded her settlement as final. Potential Presbyterians were an offshoot of a far broader group who worked for more extensive reformation within the existing structures of the church. Because they sought to purify church and society these people were dubbed "Puritans".

"The hotter sort of Protestants"

One of their number described Puritans as "the hotter sort of Protestants", a depiction that reflects the intensity of their faith (quoted, Sheils 1991: 333). Puritans devoted much of their time and energy to religious activity, sometimes spending hours in private prayer and

Bible-reading. If we are to understand their mentality we have to appreciate that God was supremely real to them. Their relationship with him was the most important thing in their lives. They internalized Calvinist teaching to a far greater extent than other people, applying the doctrine of predestination explicitly to themselves rather than seeing it as an intellectual means of understanding the mystery of God's purposes. It has been suggested that Puritans scrutinized the health of their souls as carefully as some people today watch their cholesterol levels. God's Spirit was believed to work in the lives of those whom he had chosen: thus godly living was seen as an inevitable consequence – though certainly not a cause – of election. Some introspective Puritans agonized lest their failure to walk in God's ways implied they were not members of the elect.

The popular image of Puritans is of earnest, narrow-minded people, disparagers of normal human pleasures. Their letters and journals expose a side of their personality ignored in such depictions. Moving love letters, yearning for contact with absent spouses, suggest that sexual fulfilment was readily enjoyed within marriage. Parents' journals reveal the pleasure and amusement their children gave them, anxiety for their wellbeing, and anguish at their deaths. Puritan parents struggled to accept the passing of their children as God's will, and their reflections show the part played by their faith in enabling them to come to terms with a crippling and all-too-common sorrow. Their personal writings disclose their essential humanity, the sorrows and joys they shared with other human beings.

Where Puritans differed from other people was in the source of their pleasures. There can be little doubt that they gained enormous enjoyment from "religious exercises", reading the Bible together and discussing expositions provided in recent sermons. Such meetings often took place in their houses after services or during the evenings. The Puritan family was a church in miniature: fathers fulfilled a priestly role, leading daily family prayers, catechizing their households, and exercising godly discipline (more a matter of reasoned reproof than beating), while mothers nurtured children and servants in Christian understanding. As well as gathering in each other's homes to share common enthusiasms, Puritans travelled further afield for spiritual nurture. Those who lived in parishes that did not offer a preaching ministry sometimes commuted to a neighbouring church for Sunday services. They flocked to religious lectures as others might converge on alehouses. Some groups committed themselves to a common rule of devotion, pledging mutual support and scrutiny as they sought together to live more godly lives.

Notwithstanding this tendency to develop their own sub-culture, Puritans also involved themselves in the wider community. They believed that God was active in the life of nations as well as of individuals, and assumed that his dealings with the people of Israel, recorded in the Bible, provided a model for his treatment of nations in the present. The English, who had been freed from Catholic error, were called like the Israelites of old to respond to God's mercy by walking in his ways. A nation that God had thus favoured was expected to maintain a high standard of faith and morals. Puritans insisted that obedience to the will of the creator was a universal duty. Whether or not their fellow citizens were amenable, it was incumbent on those who recognized God's call to work to realize his kingdom on earth.

Puritans were not alone in seeking to improve national standards but they approached the task as a matter of extreme urgency. If the Church of England failed to purge itself of residual Catholic practices it was inviting the wrath of God, his anger at a people who had been shown the light of true religion and chose instead to perpetuate misleading ceremonies and mindless rituals. A society that tolerated immorality and greed was similarly culpable. Puritans believed that the Bible predicted the imminent return of Christ to earth. His "second coming" would mark the end of time and God's judgement upon the world he had made. They wanted to ensure that when Christ returned their society would meet his searching demands.

Puritan reforming zeal focused upon both the church and the nation. Parish clergy were charged with the care of parishioners' souls and Puritans were anxious that they should exercise their responsibilities seriously. Only God knew who was to be saved; the task of his ministers was to ensure that the gospel message was clearly presented so that those whom God was calling could respond. Because religion was so important to them, Puritans could not bear seeing it brought into disrepute. They were horrified when drunkards staggered forward to take communion, and were very critical of bishops and clergy who did not exercise adequate discipline over the shortcomings of their flocks. The pastor's role, they believed, was to exercise fatherly correction. Equally, they were concerned that the civil authorities should act to eliminate immorality and what they saw as godlessness.

Puritan clergy supported efforts by magistrates and JPs to combat offences ranging from blasphemy to sexual misconduct and failure to work.

Activist groups who seek to impose their values on others are rarely popular. Like so many religious labels, "Puritan" was originally a term of abuse. Puritans preferred to be depicted as "the godly" or as "professors" of the faith, but these descriptions, too, evoked anger since they implied that others were irreligious, a conclusion some Puritans did not hesitate to draw. Puritan activities aroused official suspicion. Ministers were sometimes disciplined for not following the directives of the prayer book: some insisted that obedience to what they saw as the will of God had to take priority over official regulations. Particular offence was caused when Puritan clergy held extra communion services exclusively for the godly. There was anxiety lest the crowds who converged on market towns to listen to sermons got out of control. But meetings convened in Puritans' own homes were no more acceptable for they seemed to imply that official religious provision was inadequate. Puritan gatherings or "conventicles", which brought neighbours together under one roof, or drew people from different parishes across parish boundaries, were regarded as potentially subversive.

Nevertheless, Puritans were also viewed with considerable favour. Puritanism was firmly established among gentry families. Parliamentarians and leading magnates acted as patrons to Puritan magistrates and Puritan clergy, knowing that the former would not shirk their responsibilities, while the latter would perform their parish duties with exemplary thoroughness. Bishops might be aggravated by some Puritan peculiarities but they were loath to discipline men who were otherwise model incumbents, far more competent than many of their colleagues at instructing their flocks. With its insistence on accountability to God, Puritanism nurtured qualities such as thrift, diligence and hard work, which made people good citizens. Equally it discountenanced drunkenness, promiscuity and parasitical dependence upon society, which tended to act as drains upon communal resources. Notwithstanding its potential for subversion, Puritanism helped create an orderly society.

These characteristics have led many historians to associate Puritanism with the middling ranks of society. "Godly religion" appears to have flourished in market towns and cloth-manufacturing regions, hence the links that have sometimes been made between Puritan faith and the rise of capitalism. It is undoubtedly true that Puritanism nurtured qualities conducive to commercial success. But most of the rising bourgeoisie were not Puritans: even in the Kentish town of Cranbrook, long renowned as a Puritan centre, Puritans were a minority, unable to dissuade neighbours from trading and gaming on Sundays. Conversely people of both higher and humble birth were to be found in Puritan circles. The evidence to date does not permit us unambiguously to link status and faith. Age, sex and temperament may have been equally significant determinants. In so far as the young of all classes were cavalier about religious observance in Elizabeth's reign, they were unlikely to be attracted in large numbers to a devotionally demanding faith critical of popular amusements. Since Puritanism focused upon the home, the importance of women in Puritan communities is increasingly recognized. People of any age and both sexes who were naturally conscientious and hard-working may have been more readily attracted to this form of religion than happy-go-lucky types; their faith probably reinforced qualities that enabled them to get on, but they might have done so in any case.

The fact that people were labelled as "Puritans" indicates that they could be differentiated from the rest of their society. But it would be a mistake to assume that Puritans formed a totally discrete and identifiable group. Many who shared the mind-set described .above merged into the rest of the community. Those who stood out were the most vociferous and strident, constant thorns in the flesh of the ecclesiastical authorities (and maybe also of their neighbours). Many Puritans conformed to the requirements of the hierarchy, while continuing to call for the simplification of religious ceremonies and other reforms. Several Puritan aspirations were shared by the church at large. There was widespread concern among bishops, whether or not they sympathized with Puritans, to improve clerical standards. The well-supported lectures which were a feature of so many market towns did not only attract Puritans. The latter produced a disproportionate amount of the advice literature written for parents but it was purchased by a far wider readership, who presumably shared their desire to bring children up in a Christian way. What maybe differentiated "the godly" most from others was the zest, urgency and determination with which they set about these tasks. Restless and energetic, Puritans often articulated and brought about changes for which others were also working.

Prayer Book Protestants

Puritans were not the only devout people in Elizabethan England, although some of them sometimes implied that they were. There were undoubtedly some people who shared many Puritan concerns while being temperamentally disinclined to engage in the intense introspection and tightly knit fellowship characteristic of the self-styled "godly". Others, no less sincerely, found that their spiritual needs were satisfied by the liturgical provisions of the church; they had no desire to supplement these by other forms of religious activity to the extent that Puritans did. Some people in all societies express and nurture religious faith primarily through church ritual. This previously neglected group has been studied by Judith Maltby, whose unpublished thesis, from which examples below are taken, throws light on people whom historians are now labelling "parish Anglicans" or "Prayer Book Protestants".

One of the problems of studying these people is that those who were content with existing religious arrangements were less vocal and likely to leave fewer records than those who constantly called for change. This explains why Puritans dominate both contemporary records and historical accounts of Elizabethan England. But Puritan attempts to dispense with ceremonies and practices that they regarded as reminiscent of Catholicism sometimes alienated others who wished to preserve the liturgy and rites authorized in the Elizabethan settlement. The ensuing local conflicts were sometimes brought to the attention of the church courts. Parishioners of Flixton in Suffolk managed to get their vicar dismissed in 1590 for a series of offences that included refusal to wear the required vestments and to make the sign of the cross when baptizing children. They insisted on bringing their prayer books to church so that they could check that he was following the service correctly. Churchwardens of Kimcoate in Leicestershire protested because their minister was failing to read the whole prayer book service, and there were complaints that the Vicar of Sherborne in Dorset "leaveth out the exhortation and confession in the time of the communion and useth such

as himself instantly deviseth to the mislike of the communicants"
(quoted, Durston & Eales (eds) 1996: 76).

Parishioners complained to the courts not only about Puritan clergy but also about men who failed to conduct services properly
because they were lazy, drunk or otherwise occupied. The incumbent
of Manton in Lincolnshire was presented because he was too busy
playing bowls to conduct evening prayer on Wednesdays and Fridays
as he was required to do; for the same reason he failed to provide the
communion service that some of his parishioners wanted on Easter
Saturday 1577. Twenty years later, churchwardens from Folkingham
in the same county complained that their non-resident minister had
hardly conducted any communion services during the last two years.

Objections relating to the conduct of worship may have been one
way in which congregations could get rid of unpopular clergy. David
Dee of Sherborne and John Robotham of Manton had alienated their
parishioners on other counts too. Some of the ministers about whom
people complained appear to have been decidedly prickly characters,
ill able to get on with their flocks. But it would be wrong to assume
that liturgical objections were merely means to an end and did not
reflect genuine grievances. Parishioners who bothered to complain
because clergy had not conducted statutory services presumably
wanted what the latter were failing to provide – or at least some
return for their tithes. Parents, who feared that children baptized
without the sign of the cross were insufficiently protected against
evil, sometimes sought baptism outside their own parish to ensure
that the ritual was properly performed. This concern supports claims
that Prayer Book Protestants were little more than Catholics in dis-
guise, but the case must not be overstated. Initially, no doubt, many
of the people who used Cranmer's prayer book found it acceptable
because it evoked memories of pre-Reformation liturgies to which it
was indebted. But with the birth of new generations such nostalgic
loyalties were likely to decline, and fewer and fewer people can have
interpreted Cranmer's words in the light of a Catholic past. Parishioners who protested that ministers were not following the prayer
book liturgy at the end of Elizabeth's reign were unlikely to be yearning for a type of Mass last celebrated 40 years earlier. When practices reminiscent of Catholicism were reintroduced to the English
church in the 1630s, Prayer Book Protestants objected both to them
and to Puritan plans for more extensive reformation. They sought

to preserve "that order and form of divine service, which hath happily continued among us, ever since the Reformation of Religion" (quoted, Maltby 1993: 129). This mid-seventeenth-century evidence suggests that repeated use of Cranmer's prayer book had helped nurture a distinctive type of Protestant: a believer who like the Puritans affirmed the "Reformation of Religion" but unlike them was content with the settlement that Elizabeth had introduced.

Recusants and Church Papists

There were of course still some committed Catholics in England. Some of the clerics who refused to accept the Elizabethan settlement became chaplains to Catholic gentry. Others worked as itinerant priests, seeking to evade detection as they travelled round secretly conducting services in the remoter parts of the country. From 1574 missionary priests were sent to England, often young men from Catholic families who had trained at the English college recently established at Douai in northern France. Such priests ran serious risks for they could be seen as the agents of foreign powers, and specifically of the pope. Most sought refuge in gentry households, using these as bases for their mission to sustain Catholicism.

It used to be assumed that from about 1570 those who wished to preserve a Catholic heritage opted out of the life of the national church. With the passing of the old conservatively inclined priests, parish church practice became less acceptable and Catholics became "Recusants", refusing to attend authorized services. Recent research has modified this picture by identifying the existence of "Church Papists", people sympathetic to Catholicism who continued, late in the sixteenth century, occasionally to conform to the Church of England. While the term "Church Papist" was sometimes used by Puritans of anyone who attended the prayer book service without displaying their brand of personalized piety, it was also employed – no less disparagingly – by Catholic writers. Priests circulated books and pamphlets urging recusancy on people whom they saw as letting the Catholic side down by their conformity. That they did so is proof that Catholics were attending the Church of England.

Catholics who chose to conform did so for a variety of reasons. Some stressed the importance of obedience to the civil law. Some clearly preferred not to attend heretical services but were prepared to put in a token appearance when summoned before the courts. Others appear to have differentiated between the normal Sunday service, in which prayers were read, and communion services, feeling that they could attend the former without offence to their consciences but refusing to participate in what they saw as a Protestant mockery of the Mass. Others used the requirement to attend their parish churches as an opportunity to protest against the established form of religion: on Christmas Day 1595 a Lancastrian, Thomas Wintringham, refused to receive communion and "did mocke and flowte at them that did" (quoted, Walsham 1993: 91). It is significant that some Church Papists were members of Catholic families that also contained Recusants. Heads of households and their eldest sons sometimes attended Church of England services while their wives and younger children adopted the stricter recusant position. The seriousness of their Catholicism cannot be doubted, for at considerable risk some offered accommodation to visiting missionary priests and several ensured that their children received a Catholic education. Crippling fines were levied against insistent Recusants and their land might be sequestered. By occasionally attending services, landowners safeguarded their estates. Through so doing they were able to maintain priests and perpetuate the celebration of Mass within their domains. Church Papistry of this kind helped preserve Catholicism in England.

Two factors probably determined whether lay Catholics conformed to the Church of England or became Recusants: temperament and circumstance. The Church Papist position was not a psychological option for people who were unable to live with the knowledge that they had supported activities of which they believed God strongly disapproved. Other Recusants may have thrived on opposition and danger, although the extent to which they were exposed to these depended on how effectively the crown controlled their area. Catholic decisions may also have been influenced by whether or not they could hear Mass. The use of gentry households as bases for priestly activity made the priests' work possible but it also restricted it to very limited areas. Ironically Catholics who lived within reach of a jail often had more opportunities of hearing Mass than those in other parts of the country. Since prisons were privately run, how imprisoned priests were treated depended on the whim of individual jailors: some permitted them to celebrate Mass. In many places, however, the services of the Church of England were the only ones on offer, and people sympathetic to Catholicism had to decide whether to attend them or do without liturgical provision altogether. It is likely that many to whom formal religious activity was important went to their parish churches for want of any alternative.

There was always a risk, indeed a probability, that over time Church Papists would be absorbed into the Church of England. This was particularly true of those who had no opportunity to attend Mass which was so central to the maintenance and nurture of a Catholic consciousness. But those who were subsumed into the Church of England helped mould it. Church Papistry may have preserved within the national church a taste for ritual and liturgy, which ensured that it remained a broadly based community rather than one remodelled in the Puritan image.

Sectarian Protestants

As some Catholics opted out of the Church of England, so too did some radical Protestants. An early example comes from 1567 when a group of Londoners were apprehended at a meeting in Plumbers' Hall. Bishop Grindal commented

> Some London citizens of the lowest order, together with four or five ministers . . . have openly separated from us; and sometimes in private houses, sometimes in the fields, and occasionally even in ships, they have held their meetings and administered the sacraments. Besides this they have ordained ministers, elders and deacons, after their own way, and have even excommunicated some who have seceded from their church . . . The number of this sect is about two hundred, but consisting of more women than men (quoted, White 1971: 26).

Groups such as these are best described as Puritans who gave up hope of effecting reform within the Church of England. The London group emerged at the time of the vestiarian controversy. Unwilling to attend services contaminated by "idolatrous gear", people emulated the underground churches of Mary's reign, which had followed their own chosen forms of service rather than those commanded by government. They probably had no distinct theology of the church to begin with but this gradually developed as they looked for scriptural models and worked out how to order their communities. Their thinking was articulated by leaders such as Robert Browne in Norwich and Henry Barrow in London, after whom groups came to be named. Their experience led them to believe that true churches comprised only people who had personally responded to Christ. A church was formed when a group of such people made a binding commitment or "covenant" to seek God together. Effective discipline was regarded as one of the hallmarks of a biblically based church: practice followed New Testament suggestions that congregations should gently remonstrate with those who failed to live up to their calling, expelling the impenitent from their fellowship. Thus, authority in the church was exercised by the community of believers, not by some externally imposed hierarchy of bishops or by the secular powers. In the opinion of those who separated from the Church of England, neither of these had sufficed to keep that church free from corruption.

People moved from Puritan conformity into Separatist communities, and some (including Robert Browne) moved back again, but there were two fundamental differences between the two positions. Puritans had no doubt that the Church of England was imperfect and in need of further reform but they saw it as essentially a true church through which God was working: notwithstanding its propensity for vestments and ceremonies, it was a bastion of anti-Catholicism; on the all-important doctrine of salvation it maintained an impeccably Calvinist stance. Whereas most Puritans were prepared to work within a church that had bishops, the break-away groups could see no biblical justification for an ecclesiastical hierarchy. Continuing popish corruptions of this sort rendered the Church of England a false church, from which Separatists believed they were bound to separate if they were to remain true to the gospel. By implication they equated it with the Church of Rome.

The second difference was even more significant. Like almost all English people of their day Puritans instinctively accepted the idea of a national church to which everyone belonged. Most probably found it impossible to conceive of any other arrangement. After the Reformation as before, every English person belonged to a parish and was by birth a member of the church in England. Belonging to the church was as universal and inescapable as citizenship. To opt out of the established church (when there was no opt-out clause) and establish alternative communities as the Separatists did threatened the concept of a nation as an undivided entity. Unlike Recusants, Protestant Separatists were not necessarily associated with foreign powers but they were seen as dangerously subversive. Some fled persecution to the safety of the Netherlands, many were imprisoned, and a few leaders including Henry Barrow were executed during the last decades of the century on charges of sedition.

Separatism as such was very rare. Given the enormity both psychologically and practically of the decision to break away from the church to which everyone belonged, it is not surprising that members of other Protestant sects continued to attend parish church services. One such group was the Family of Love, which owed its origin to a Dutch refugee, Hendrik Niclaes. It is not easy to determine from Niclaes' translated writings exactly what he and his followers believed. Their faith was not a matter of doctrinal understanding but of mystical identification with God. Through intense meditation they sought spiritual transformation and a sense of oneness with the divine, in Niclaes' words to be "godded with god" (quoted, Marsh 1994: 20). Members of the Family of Love met together in small groups to read the Bible and Niclaes' works. Itinerant leaders travelled round, keeping groups in touch with each other and acting as mobile librarians. We know of Familists in the counties around Cambridgeshire, in London, Surrey and Devon, and there may have been more. Zealous Puritans pursued them vigorously, fearing that Niclaes' claims of personal inspiration and his followers' enthusiasm for his writings distracted attention from the greater authority of the Bible. Familists seemed to downplay the uniqueness of Christ by suggesting that others could achieve a comparable state of perfection in this life. Except for a few years in the 1570s when they attracted government attention, Familists did not suffer much formal constraint. Their inward-looking mystical faith may have appealed to the introspective who were unlikely to attract official attention. Since they refrained from obvious proselytizing and attended their parish churches, they were rarely brought before the church courts. Their willingness to conform enabled the Family of Love to survive, but like Church Papists they ran the risk of absorption into the Church of England and the loss of their distinctive principles. Snippets of evidence suggest there may have been other such groups.

An accommodating church

In Elizabeth's reign there was a great deal of religious activity in addition to the authorized services of the parish churches. There were meetings of Protestant sects, such as Brownists, Barrowists and Familists. There was the celebration of Mass in secluded villages, gentry households and even in prisons. Far more commonly there were town lectures and a multiplicity of religious gatherings, some in homes, some outdoors, some in churches, and some in other communal meeting places, organized by Puritans who could never have enough of such exercises. Religious itinerants of different persuasions travelled the country distributing literature, preaching and seeking to convert.

It can be argued that since the Church of England embraced the whole population it had to be fairly broadly based. The more rigorous Puritans disagreed with this and sought to impose their own stricter creed on the population at large. But they stood little chance of success. Paradoxically it was the comparative liberality of the established church that enabled them to stay within it. Had they been unable to supplement official religious provision with their own voluntary activities far more would probably have turned to Separatism. In later centuries the label "nonconformist" denoted Separatists who opted out of the Church of England. It is significant that in histories of the sixteenth century the term is used of people within the Church of England who did not fully conform to its liturgical requirements. Some ministers ignored rites and formularies without being brought before the courts. Men such as George Gifford, who was dismissed from his charge for nonconformity, were re-employed as lecturers. Their job was to preach not conduct prayer book services. Others became private chaplains. In these ways hard-line Puritans were able to avoid involvement in liturgies they disliked and remain within the established church.

Official toleration of a wide variety of religious practices can be attributed in part to the difficulty of exercising control, but that in itself is an inadequate explanation. Elizabeth and many of her bishops and officials were primarily concerned to maintain order, and this was better achieved by allowing some leeway for unofficial activity than by driving people into outright opposition. The authorities were more concerned with conformity than orthodoxy, assuming that the former guaranteed the latter: providing people were willing to abide by official requirements there was relatively little enquiry into what they actually believed. This makes it difficult for historians to analyze types of faith in the sixteenth century, but there is clear evidence of diversity. The fact that Church Papists and Familists could both be found at court testifies to the variety of beliefs that were effectively tolerated within the Elizabethan Church of England.

CHAPTER FIVE

Religion and popular culture in the late sixteenth century

Popular culture, deeply entwined with the beliefs and practices of the Catholic Church, was bound to be affected by the religious changes of the sixteenth century. But the Reformation was not an isolated force destroying a "Merrie England" that might otherwise have survived intact. Culture is dynamic, a process, not a static pattern of customs. Some practices were already in decline before the Reformation. At the same time the advent of printing introduced new forms of popular expression. The Reformation was one of a number of influences, albeit a very important one, contributing to an evolving cultural landscape.

Challenges to communal festivity

Official attempts to purge the national faith of superstition profoundly affected group identities and communal activity. Parochial clubs that existed to raise money for candles burnt before images lost their *raison d'être*, as did lay fraternities that had provided recreation for the living while catering for the welfare of the dead. Liturgical ceremonies that had colourfully and dramatically marked the passage of the church year were either abolished or survived in muted form. By demolishing shrines Henry put an immediate end to pilgrimages (and to the associated souvenir trades) while Elizabeth forbad parish processions save those at rogationtide. Bishops' visitation records suggest that the latter no longer expressed corporate togetherness to the extent they once had. Elizabeth had ordered that the beating of the bounds should in future take place without banners and vestments. Since the rite derived from Catholic practice and the modifications were sometimes ignored, some parishioners complained that its continued observation was popish; others objected when parish officials neglected to hold the processions.

Other once popular customs, banned by Edward and revived under Mary, survived into Elizabeth's reign but appear gradually to have declined in popularity. In some parishes it had been customary to maintain a "plough light" in church and to observe "Plough Sunday" just before ploughing started in January. This probably involved the blessing of ploughs, maybe brought into church for the purpose, and was often followed by revelry and the dragging of ploughs round the streets to raise money. Another common way of obtaining funds for a local church was through church ales, which provided scope not only for drinking but for feasting and fun. During the Elizabethan period fewer parishes seem to have observed Plough Monday festivities than before, while church ales died out in several regions albeit continuing elsewhere.

One of the reasons for the decline in such practices was a change in fund-raising methods. Whereas ales had once been the major source of parish revenue, now they merely supplemented it. In an age of inflation parishes chose to rely more on the levying of rates and on rents for seats in church than on the decreasing and variable income obtainable from communal festivity. Another reason was a growing concern for public order. Like church ales many traditional recreations had long been occasions for extreme licence: the twelve days of revelry at Christmas, the sports and drinking following the feasts of St Philip and St James on May Day, the start of summer, and the bonfires and games at the midsummer commemoration of St John the Baptist could all easily get out of hand. Corporations were making some attempt to control them even before the Reformation.

A degree of disorder was part of the purpose of some of these rites for they provided a form of institutionalized indiscipline, an explicit and deliberate reversal of accepted behaviour. At Christmas, towns, noble households and colleges sometimes appointed Lords of Misrule, mock rulers to whom those normally in authority became temporarily subservient. The dressing-up of a boy as a bishop on St Nicholas' Day similarly gave people the opportunity to deride established authority: in cathedrals the bishop often presided over services and preached a sermon; in some parishes he was the centre of a money-raising procession, solemnly blessing his elders in emulation of ecclesiastical dignitaries. On Hock Monday, eight days after Easter, gangs of men captured women and demanded ransoms for charity for their release, while the following day the roles were reversed so that for once power was in female hands. These regular, semi-ritualized opportunities to go against the norm served to release tension, and made it less likely that frustration with the established order would erupt in more damaging ways. Thus traditional society maintained its structure and taboos by permitting and even encouraging people to flout them on fixed and circumscribed occasions.

These ways of maintaining stability lost some of their viability in the course of the sixteenth century because of a rapid increase in population and the escalating proportion of people under 20. The inherent risk that institutionalized disorder might develop into more serious, potentially uncontrollable disorder increased to unacceptable levels. Riots and rebellions often took place during the major festivals: the western rising of 1549 erupted during the celebrations at Whitsuntide (the commemoration of the gift of God's Spirit to Jesus' disciples). Municipal corporation records reveal that in the course of Elizabeth's reign town after town dropped its sponsorship of games and maypole dancing, bonfires, plays and pageants. Instead at May, Whitsun and midsummer the tumultuous and raucous informality of spontaneous sport and traditional merrymaking began to give way to organized races and formal shows of men in armour. This is not to suggest that old practices disappeared entirely: Shrove Tuesday, a day of carnival and feasting on the eve of Lent, occasioned riots well into the seventeenth century. While many communities continued to enjoy pageants and bonfires, in London and some other towns participatory festivities seem gradually to have been superseded by more easily controllable audience-based recreation.

Among the casualties of this change were the mystery plays, traditionally performed in the streets by guilds of craftsmen during various religious festivals. The demise of this popular form of entertainment was accelerated by a change in Protestant attitudes. In the early days of the Reformation Protestants had been concerned to purge the plays of popish elements, not to ban them, and a Protestant drama had emerged to combat their influence in kind. But during the last quarter of the century the whole concept of religious drama was called into question. The traditional intermingling of bawdiness and religion was now seen to be irreverent; the word of God deserved thoughtful not flippant treatment. To dress people up as biblical figures or as the deity was at best mockery, at worst idolatry. Drama on biblical themes was increasingly deemed to be blasphemous and by the end of Elizabeth's reign it had virtually disappeared.

The "hotter sort of Protestants" challenged other popular amusements. Among the ten commandments given to the ancient Israelites was the order to keep the sabbath day holy. Puritans came to believe that the Christian equivalent, Sunday, should be devoted to religious activity and therefore opposed the games and dancing that regularly took place on that day. But mixed dancing was no more acceptable on any other day of the week for it was deemed to be conducive to lust and sexual misdemeanour. This partly explains Puritan antagonism to May Day celebrations: contemporary accounts suggest that normal sexual restraints may have been cast aside in a night of revelry, possibly dating back to the old orgiastic fertility festival that marked the start of summer. While pre-Freudian people might not have identified maypoles as phallic symbols, Puritans associated them with illicit sexual activity. But dancing round the maypole also evoked images of the Israelites cavorting round a man-made golden calf and thereby reverting to idolatry. The Hebrew Bible resounded with complaints against the heathen habit of venerating stones, trees and fabricated representations of deities. In Puritan minds the May Day festivities were part of an old Catholic world in which celebration centred on artefacts, natural objects and images rather than the one true God. Maypoles evoked a host of antagonistic feelings and some Puritans tried to cut them down.

We cannot know how far civic opposition to traditions such as maypole dancing were Puritan-inspired and how far they reflected the need to preserve order. Disturbances in London on May Day 1517, long before the emergence of a Protestant ethic, caused the city authorities to ban the erection of a maypole. While some historians have regarded late Elizabethan attempts to enforce sexual morality as Puritan in motivation, others point out that increasing readiness to report sexual misdemeanours was not restricted to areas of Puritan strength. Concern about the cost to communities of children who had no acknowledged fathers to support them was widespread. It seems reasonable to conclude that while Protestantism presented a significant challenge to several popular festivities, its advent coincided with other developments conducive to the same end. It provided powerful motivation and influential backing for attempts to control communal activities which in some cases were already under threat for other reasons. Many traditional forms of merrymaking survived notwithstanding the change in climate, but by the end of the century they were less thriving and less widespread than they had been at its start.

The secularization of popular culture

One way of assessing religious influence on these developments is to compare what was happening in England with similar changes taking place elsewhere in Europe. Several historians have suggested that Protestantism led ultimately to the secularization of popular culture. In reaction to the Reformation continental Catholics sought to purge their church of abuses but they defined these differently from Protestants. The leaders of the Catholic Counter-Reformation objected to apocryphal stories about saints that distorted the respect properly directed to them; Protestants objected to any veneration of the saints. In 1559 Norwich's pageant in celebration of St George was discontinued, but as a sop to public opinion the organizers agreed that the dragon, "Old Snap", might still make an appearance, a practice that persisted for nearly 300 years. Peter Burke comments, "the reform of popular culture in Catholic Augsburg meant showing St George without the dragon; in Protestant Norwich it meant showing the dragon without St George" (Burke 1978: 216).

Other changes were similarly conducive to secularization. The organized sports and shows that constituted the emergent civic culture lacked the religious redolence of the old festivities. Protestant suspicion of religious drama meant that theatrical production became totally divorced from the church, once its major sponsor. Reacting against the belief that the cross merited worship, Protestants destroyed wayside and market crosses that might tempt people to idolatry. But this meant that people who lacked deep religious convictions were no longer prompted by the sights around them momentarily to recall the things of God. With the dissolution of religious orders and the closing-down of chantry chapels there were far fewer people wearing religious dress. As reminders of another world ceased to impinge on people's attention so piety, no longer rooted in the tangible, was less obviously part of common life.

Some traditional customs survived but lost their religious significance. While Palm Sunday rituals were banned the practice of gathering willow on the Sunday before Easter persisted. Drawing on nineteenth- and twentieth-century folklore collections, Ronald Hutton has shown that "going a palming" or, its northern version, "going a palmsoning" variously involved processing with flowers and greenery to some communal gathering point, or decorating homes. In Dorset and Nottinghamshire the custom of blessing candles in church at Candlemas seems to have been transmuted into offering candles as gifts on 2 February. In these and other instances practices outlawed from church appear to have been privatized, domesticated and consequently desacralized (Hutton 1995).

The gradual nature of this transition towards greater secularity needs to be emphasized. The records of church courts provide clear evidence that some popular religious customs continued despite official disapproval. During the 1560s church bells were regularly rung on All Saints' night to comfort souls in purgatory. Bishops were still condemning the practice 20 years later, implying that it had not altogether died out. By permitting the continuation of rogationtide processions, Elizabeth made possible the perpetuation of the old beliefs associated with them. The new regulations were designed to divest the rite of its magical elements; ministers were encouraged to pray for good weather and a successful harvest as they beat the bounds, but were not permitted to use processional crosses that might be construed as magically bringing blessing to the fields through which they passed. Nevertheless in some areas crosses were carved on trees in place of the wayside images at which processions had traditionally paused for prayer and readings, and the custom of reading the Gospel over the crops continued. As Puritans recognized, the only way effectively to desacralize the rogationtide processions was to abolish them altogether.

The development of the calendar reflects the persistence of traditional religious modes of thought as well as growing secularization. Attempts had been made to reduce the number of holy days as early as the 1530s as much for economic as for religious reasons. The harvest season was largely cleared of religious celebrations, and the number of saints' days on which work could be set aside was drastically reduced. But while worshipping saints was condemned, the Elizabethan settlement legitimized their commemoration. Popular almanacs and later editions of the Elizabethan prayer book listed not only (in red print) holy days on which people were expected to refrain from labour and attend church but also, more circumspectly in black, some of the older saints' days that no longer carried exemption from work. Thus the old ecclesiastical calendar continued to provide landmarks in people's perceptions of time. The four terms of the legal year and the days on which civil and church courts met were still known by the old religious names and these were even used in recording parliamentary statutes. Fairs continued to be called after the saints on whose days they had traditionally met. Force of habit kept awareness of the medieval calendar alive long after affection for the saints who featured in it had declined. At the same time a new dynastic calendar was superimposed upon the old religious one. David Cressy (1989) has shown how, as time progressed, bonfires and bells were used not only to mark religious festivals, but also to commemorate events such as the accession of Elizabeth on 17 November. During her reign residual religious modes of thought co-existed alongside movement towards greater secularity.

Protestant culture

Historians who stress the secularizing impact of Protestantism sometimes overlook continuities with the past: the extent to which the church and religious practices still occupied a central role in community life. As in the past everyone was required to pay tithe and various other levies to the church, including a new charge for the purchase of communion wine. Parish churches remained local rallying-points. Fire-fighting equipment and weapons were stored in them and parish chests sometimes served as repositories for important documents that individuals were loath to store in wooden houses which might easily go up in flames. Church bells were rung as alarums and at times of celebration. Local officers were often appointed and accounts agreed in the churchyard. The church door was the local notice board on which rhymes and caricatures of members of the community might be nailed. On Christmas Day 1603 a "true bede-roll of the whores known in Warminster" was fixed to a church door with the request that the parish officers deal with the delinquents (quoted, Ingram 1987: 165). Sexual misdemeanours and slander were among the offences over which church courts retained jurisdiction. Those who were convicted were still sometimes required to perform public penances, occasionally in the market place but normally in church. Dressed in white sheets they stood before the congregation throughout the service, publicly confessed their sin, and listened to a homily directed against it. The penalties imposed by church courts paralleled the humiliating rituals (such as riding backwards on a horse) to which popular custom subjected those who offended against society's sexual norms. Thus the church continued to be involved in attempts to maintain social conformity and communal wellbeing.

The local church remained the focus for important events in people's lives: births, marriages and deaths. A month after her confinement it was customary for a woman to come to church for a service of blessing and purification marking her reinstatement (after recuperation) into the community. The church service was generally followed by a feast at which the newly churched woman celebrated with her friends. This practice of "churching" women was modified to conform to Protestant belief. Before the Reformation the religious ceremony involved sprinkling with holy water to cleanse the contamination of childbirth. The 1552 prayer book deleted all reference to purification and omitted the use of holy water. Instead emphasis was laid upon thanksgiving. Churching placed the woman (not her baby) at the centre of attention and remained a very popular practice, sought by the vast majority of women of all classes notwithstanding the fee involved.

Other traditional customs underwent more radical transformation into Protestant form. The Catholic Church had designated fixed times during the year as fast days to aid personal reflection and purification. Protestants objected to these partly because they often preceded feast days on which saints were venerated and partly because they seemed to be yet another means of trying to earn God's favour. But fasting had good biblical credentials. It was a way of focusing attention on important matters without the distraction of comfort-eating. In Elizabethan England national fast days were called at times of crisis, when plague struck or invasion threatened, to enable the nation to lament and turn away from sins that seemed to be provoking divine judgement. Puritans went beyond this and held additional unauthorized fasts as part of their religious discipline. These were corporate ways of prompting awareness of human sinfulness and divine mercy. By meditating on their failings and opening themselves to God's power to overcome them, Puritans hoped to take a step forward on the path to godly living. Puritan fast days were often mammoth preaching festivals: in Southill, Bedfordshire, in 1603 there were six hours' worth of sermons, presumably interspersed with psalm-singing, prayer and meditation. Such a day normally ended with a communal meal, paralleling the feast day celebrations that had succeeded fasts in Catholic England.

The cycle of the church year as observed by Catholics was similarly transmuted into a different Puritan form. The Catholic Church seemed to Puritans to hallow days that God had not sanctioned. According to the biblical account of creation, God rested on the seventh day. The ten commandments ordered that no work should be performed on it. Puritans maintained that the divinely ordained pattern was one of working days punctuated by a weekly sabbath, on which as the Elizabethan era progressed they laid increasing emphasis. But Puritans like Catholics enjoyed a multiplicity of other occasions for religious observance, which they fitted in alongside work. Whereas lay people in Catholic England had founded chantries and funded free-lance priests to say Mass, now the affluent supported preachers. If lecturers were the Protestant equivalent of friars, preachers relatively free of ecclesiastical controls, then the market days on which lectures were given replicated the old saints' days. People present in a town on a lecture day would be as aware of the crowds thronging to a lecture as their predecessors had been of the crowds joining a procession or jostling to see the casketted host. Indeed Puritans often marched in convoy to a lecture singing psalms as they went. The psalms were set to lively tunes (replaced by more sober ones in the seventeenth century) and sermons could be highly dramatic performances. Historians are thus beginning to question the assumption that a religion based upon the word lacked public spectacle and appeal.

The most dramatic public spectacles were perhaps the dying speeches of convicted felons made to assembled crowds just before they were hanged. From the point of view of the authorities it was highly desirable that they should acknowledge their guilt thereby reaffirming the public order against which they had offended. (Some provided added thrills by asserting their innocence.) Protestant ministers were anxious to bring about eleventh-hour repentance believing that as Christ had forgiven the penitent thief who died on the cross beside him so he would forgive latter-day penitents. Faced with the imminence of death prisoners were psychologically vulnerable to importunate urgings to repent in the hope of being whisked from the gallows to eternal bliss. The sight of a penitent criminal testifying to faith in God before compliantly accepting the proper retribution for his or her offence was a powerful evangelistic tool. Crowds gathered to watch executions while popular murder pamphlets transmitted accounts of last-minute conversions and "good" deaths to a far wider audience.

Catholic priests, incarcerated in the same prisons, were in a strong position to compete for the souls of those about to be hanged: some criminals challenged spectators' expectations by blaming their disordered lives on the heresy of Protestantism from which they had been rescued in the nick of time. But such Catholic claims were more than offset by widely diffused anti-Catholic propaganda. Popular anti-Catholicism was a novel feature of the emergent Protestant culture. Its roots lay in a long-standing aversion to foreigners, reinforced by Mary's marriage to the unpopular Philip of Spain. The growing association of Protestantism and patriotism was strengthened by threats of Spanish invasion and suspicion of French collusion with Mary Queen of Scots, the Catholic heir to the throne. Foreign Catholic rulers were regarded as lackeys of the pope, who was explicitly depicted in Foxe's book of martyrs as the anti-Christ, the ultimate antithesis and opponent of Christ. It was an easy step for people who had long seen the world as a cosmic battle between good and evil to view the pope and hence his followers as partisans on the diabolic side. Foxe provided a Protestant interpretation of history, vividly illustrated by pictures of burning and torture. These were capable of inspiring anti-Catholic sentiments in those least capable of reading. While the lower orders might not have had direct access to Foxe's book they were able to buy ballads that popularized his accounts of Marian martyrs. These too were adorned with lurid woodcuts. Thus heroic and gory stories of contemporary Protestant martyrs gradually replaced traditional graphic accounts of the agonizing deaths of Catholic saints. The 1569 rising of northern Catholic earls and the pope's excommunication of Elizabeth the following year prompted a host of anti-Catholic ballads, some replicating Foxe's perception of recent history, others mocking Catholic practices and papal pretensions: "A balade of a priest that loste his nose, For sayinge of masse, as I suppose".

The production of cheap religious prints, hawked around the country by pedlars, introduced a new dimension into popular culture. Thousands of copies of ballads were sold in the second half of the sixteenth century at between a halfpenny and a penny each. Tessa Watt has calculated that at least a third of those recorded in the Stationers' Registers in the middle of Elizabeth's reign were on religious and moral themes. They were printed by firms that produced a miscellaneous range of material. This suggests that their concerns were commercial rather than evangelistic and that they published what people wanted to buy (Watt 1991: 42–52). It seems reasonable to assume that, to some extent at least, the ballads reflected popular taste.

Early ballads often paraphrased biblical stories thereby familiarizing the public with them – or with sensationalized versions of them. Like the mystery plays before them they described scriptural characters in humorous, sometimes titillating ways. The Bible was full of dramatic stories capable of evoking popular interest. Among those reproduced most frequently were an account of King David's infatuation with a soldier's wife ("he spide a Lady faire ... She stood within a pleasant Bower, all naked, for to wash her there") and "A new ditty, shewing the wonderfull miracles of our Lord". By the end of Elizabeth's reign Protestant writers were ceasing to produce new ballads of this kind, presumably for the same reasons that they stopped writing religious drama. But existing ballads continued to be reproduced, sold and presumably sung.

Many of the themes explored in cheap prints were inherited from the Catholic past. Ballads gave aphoristic expression to basic moral precepts, inveighed against contemporary wickedness, and reflected an abiding preoccupation with death, the ensuing judgement, heaven and hell. Calls to repentance and urgings to avoid the pain of hell were common as in "The pittiful lamentation of a damned soul" or a ballad that began "Remember man both night and day, Thou must nedes die, there is no nay".

This continuity with the past is not surprising. Because Protestants opposed Catholics so vehemently we tend to think of the two creeds as starkly antagonistic and to forget how much they had in common. Both believed in a cosmic battle between the forces of good and evil, and drew copiously on biblical material. Both focused on a God who oversaw human affairs, expected moral behaviour from the people he had created, and would ultimately determine their eternal destiny. Thus the Protestant culture that was emerging in the course of Elizabeth's reign perpetuated beliefs and attitudes shared with Catholic predecessors. Rites of passage were modified into Protestant form but retained features from the past. New Protestant practices took over the role of Catholic conventions they were replacing. The effect of this was to create a form of culture that was rooted in what had gone before and yet had a very different texture. This can be seen in popular prints that fused inherited religious attitudes with new emphases: anti-Catholic sentiment, occasional illustrations of saving faith, and the celebration of Protestant martyrs in place of the saints who had played so central a role in traditional culture.

Pictures and print

One of the main differences assumed to exist between Catholic and Protestant culture derives from the emphasis Protestants placed on the written word. In England the introduction of a vernacular Bible was accompanied by the impassioned destruction of images, once seen as books for the unlearned. The widespread production of printed texts at the time of the Reformation is presumed to mark a transition from a pictorial to a verbal culture, from images to concepts, and from oral to written discourse.

Recent studies have challenged this account. A stark distinction between spoken and written communication does not adequately reflect the reality of late sixteenth-century experience. The boundary between oral and literary culture was hazy: printed ballads, sung on village greens and streets, were passed on in vocal as well as written form. At all levels of society learning to read was an oral experience, a skill acquired through rote-learning, memorization and recitation. Moreover, reading was taught separately from writing and historians of literacy are now convinced that far more people could read than write. Some may have been able to cope with some scripts and not with others: it has been suggested that the black letter script used for ballads and government proclamations may have been designed for those of very limited reading ability.

While the advent of printing brought about an explosion of literary activity, this did not necessarily mean that pictures were replaced by words or images by concepts. On the contrary, cheap prints combined the verbal with the pictorial. As time went by broadsides, productions on a single sheet of paper, were increasingly decorated with pictures and motifs. These were pinned up on cottage walls as a form of household decoration. Word diagrams were also displayed. Pedlars sold printed paper replicas of physical objects such as gloves, in their material form popular courtship gifts. Each finger listed a new year resolution, while virtues and vices were catalogued on opposing palms. Towards the end of the century schematic tables of advice and rules began to be produced, in which pictures and emblems were juxtaposed with diagrammatic word arrangements, visual aids to memory stuck on to cottage walls.

In churches pictorial embellishment had largely been replaced by mural inscriptions of biblical verses. This practice was domesticated in the form of black letter texts etched on door jambs and painted on walls as friezes and decorative panels. The alehouses in which they were most commonly seen also contained wall-paintings on cloth or paper, as did some houses and cottages. Like the ballads, post-Reformation wall-paintings featured figures from the Hebrew Bible and some popular New Testament stories such as that of the prodigal son. These may have been acceptable even to stricter Protestants because unlike the old pictures of saints they would not have evoked veneration. Nor, when displayed in domestic environments, were they liable to distract from the simple reading of the word, a reason for the exclusion of pictures from church. But even in churches visual images survived on a small scale: moulded figures high on church roofs and tiny stained-glass pictures were too distant to be reverenced, and because of the difficulty and cost of removal were often left in place. It has been suggested that the cramped illustrations on broadsides replicated in homes the images at which people distantly peered in church. Thus pictorial communication survived the Reformation to a far greater extent than was once assumed, challenging the assumption that there was a major shift from an image-based to a conceptual mental world.

Protestantism focused on the Bible, but this did not mean that only the educated had access to religious ideas. It was after all a religion of the word, and words could be preached – and sung – as well as read. They could also operate as images: entering a house people might touch the words "Fear God" inscribed on the lintel as a form of protection. The vehicle of the all-powerful word of God, the Bible itself became talismanic, a Protestant holy object, to which old habits of veneration were transferred. The illiterate touched it reverently while some who could read opened it at random in the belief that God would speak to them through the verse on which their eye alighted.

The print revolution meant that in the course of the sixteenth century the written word became less alien to uneducated people. Printed texts became a new component of popular culture. The subject-matter of broadside prints, which the people of England purchased in vast quantities and stuck on their walls, reveals that religious values and themes remained deeply entrenched in their culture. Tessa Watt, to whose work the last few pages are indebted, comments:

> We must not think of religion as the exclusive preserve of the church, but look for ways in which "religious" beliefs in the broadest sense were encountered throughout local society: in popular songs, in cloths on alehouse walls, in tables posted up in cottages, or in accounts of grisly executions chanted out in the market-places (Watt 1991: 328).

Religion in this broad sense was still part of everyday life.

Protestantism, astrology and magic

Elizabethan people of all levels of society believed that the universe was suffused with supernatural forces. In this respect late sixteenth-century communities bore far more resemblance to earlier societies than to our own. Eighteenth- and nineteenth-century historians tended to see Protestantism as the first step towards a more recognizably modern world, an essentially rationalist faith, out of tune with popular credulity. This interpretation drew credence from anti-Catholic propaganda which depicted Protestantism as a rational rather than a superstitious faith. But Elizabethan Protestants were not rationalists; they saw signs of divine activity all around them. The Puritan who just missed being struck by lightning attributed this deliverance to God's care or, in Protestant terminology, his providence. Using different language, murder pamphlets depicted the world as an arena of divine judgement: wrongs were supernaturally righted when criminals were stopped from escaping by bad weather or by the miraculous laming of their horses; corpses were believed to sweat blood in the presence of those who had killed them. Broadside literature testified to popular conviction that prodigies such as the earthquake that struck in 1580, the birth of handicapped infants and deformed animals all signalled divine displeasure.

Given widespread interest in the cosmic meaning of temporal happenings it is not surprising that astrology was a popular science. A new star identified in 1572 was interpreted as presaging the second coming of Christ, in the same way that a star had signalled his birth in Bethlehem. Intense excitement and apprehension was evoked in 1583 by the conjunction of Saturn and Jupiter, interpreted by astrologers as a sign that the end was at hand. Expectations of the end were also aroused by Protestant fascination with the apocalyptic writings of the Bible which vividly describe the final conflict between good and evil. The momentous religious events of the sixteenth century reinforced the conviction that humankind was living through the last days.

These various perceptions were brought together in popular form in almanacs. Describing cosmic portents, the compilers issued repeated warnings about the imminence of death and urged people to repent. Essentially calendars, almanacs listed religious festivals and the biblical passages to be read in church services, along with astrological information about days on which it was lucky or unlucky to perform certain agricultural tasks, to let blood, or engage in other medical interventions. There was a variety of reactions within the Church of England to such predictions. Some ministers practised astrology arguing that heavenly bodies were agents of God's will: comets were God's merciful way of alerting people to impending judgement, of giving the nation the opportunity to repent and therefore avert the evil that would otherwise befall them. But there was also much clerical suspicion. There was a risk that criminals might blame their anti-social behaviour on the stars. Puritans were particularly critical of astrology because it attempted to probe divine mysteries and in so doing set up an alternative deterministic system to their own. Astrology seemed to usurp the role of divine providence.

A similar gap between the supernaturalist beliefs of the godly and those of the rest of society can be identified in their attitudes to black and white magic. There was widespread belief in witchcraft in six-teenth-century Europe. Suffering from mishaps thought to be caused by witches, terrified people brought accusations against neighbours in a desperate attempt to protect themselves from further *malefi-cium*, the inflicting of evil. Protestant ministers in England as else-where acknowledged that there were witches who gave themselves to the devil, but warned people against blaming witchcraft for every-thing that went wrong in their lives. Puritans believed that everything that happened was ordained by God. Suffering might be sent, as to Job in the Bible, as a test of faith, or it might be a punishment for wrongdoing. Writers such as Henry Holland and George Gifford stressed that the proper response to misfortune was to see what God was saying through it. By blaming witches people were avoiding the self-scrutiny that Puritan pastors regarded as desirable. They were externalizing rather than internalizing causes of ill.

In comparison with other countries there were relatively few prose-cutions for witchcraft in England. The fear witchcraft aroused was intense, comparable to that evoked today by serial rapists or killers, but it was not a central concern in most people's lives. In *A dialogue concerning witches and witchcraft* of 1593 Gifford was equally critic-al of the "other sort of Witches, whome the people call cunning men and wise women", magical practitioners whose intentions were kindly not malevolent (quoted, Clark 1990: 65). It is impossible to assess how many of these cunning folk there were but it appears that they were both numerous and popular. Knowledgeable (or "cun-ning") in magical lore, they used herbal medicines, charms, repeated recitation of Latin and sometimes English prayers, and the balancing of sieves and shears as a means of divination, to assist those who con-sulted them. People turned to them for protection against witchcraft, for healing, for guidance when faced by important decisions and for aid in finding lost goods and detecting thieves. Accounts of how they operated suggest that they were psychologically skilled; by adroit questioning they enabled their clients to articulate their own suspi-cions of who had harmed them or what was wrong. While they pre-dated the Reformation, the demand for their services may have increased after it. In Catholic England objects and persons hallowed by the church had been regarded as vehicles through which God's power was exercised on earth. Deprived of the opportunities of seeking healing at shrines of saints and of using holy objects as talismans against ill, the needy turned instead to alternative sources of aid.

Puritan opposition to such activities derived partly from the fact that they were indicted in the Bible. They also offended against God's sovereignty. Puritans stressed that the supernatural could not be manipulated and so opposed any rite, whether Catholic or magical, that implied that God could be induced to act at human behest. Their antagonism to folk magic paralleled their antagonism to what they saw as ecclesiastical magic, the use of special words and objects to harness divine power. The proper course of action in times of need was to pray: people should beseech God, in his mercy, to grant their requests, while recognizing that it was up to him whether he did so or not. But prayer in the hope that God might graciously answer did not have the same popular appeal as methods of dealing with misfortune that seemed to have a more guaranteed outcome. It is not surprising that the populace continued to seek the remedies and charms proffered by cunning folk, turning more and more to magical practitioners for help they might once have found within the church.

The Elizabethan injunctions of 1559 ordered that "no persons shall use charms, sorceries, enchantments, witchcraft, soothsaying, or any such like devilish device, nor shall resort at any time to the same for counsel or help" (quoted, Gee & Hardy 1910: 432–3). Nevertheless, cunning folk were rarely brought before the courts and when they were they tended to receive lenient treatment. Church court prosecutions arose when local people presented their neighbours; those who practised magical arts were often valued by their communities. By denying that holy objects were invested with magical powers the reformers divorced religion and magic but parishioners continued to combine the two. In 1582 a cunning man was appointed churchwarden in Chelmsford, while not long after the churchwardens of Thatcham in Berkshire asked a cunning woman to find out who had stolen the cloth from their communion table. Historians of Puritan America have shown how faith even in that strict society was infused with magical beliefs and practices, and the same was almost certainly true of Elizabethan England, less subject to Puritan control. Richard Godbeer comments "Like many English men and women before them . . . colonists took disparate beliefs and mixed them together in order to concoct for themselves a workable, if intellectually untidy, mental world" (Godbeer 1992: 54; cf. Hall 1990).

This mental world cut across class boundaries. Elizabeth consulted an astrologer, one of her close confidants, before setting the date of her coronation. Lady Arabella Stuart took account of phases of the moon when cutting her hair. In delineating what he saw as the pernicious influence of cunning people, Gifford recorded that "the woman at R. H. by report hath some weeke fourtie come unto her, and many of them not of the meaner sort" (quoted, Macfarlane 1970: 120). The wide-ranging appeal of astrological and magical beliefs makes it difficult to sustain claims that the Reformation introduced a gulf between an elite religious culture and a popular magical culture. The gulf that it did induce appears to have been more between the godly and the rest: between those who interpreted everything in terms of God's providence, regarding other supernaturalist claims as threats to their own creed, and those who drew upon a more eclectic range of beliefs, religious, astrological and magical, to cope with the eventualities of life. But it would be a mistake to assume that even the faith of the godly was necessarily homogeneous. The American evidence suggests that Puritan church members sometimes resorted to magical techniques without showing any sense of inconsistency. Did lay people in England associated with Puritan communities do so too? The popular culture of Elizabethan England was in Godbeer's words an "untidy mental world": in a constant state of evolution, it was a hybrid fusion of the old and the new, the religious and the magical, a medley of beliefs and customs out of which people from different levels of society and with differing religious commitments made sense of their experience.

Conclusion

The title of this book, *From Catholic to Protestant*, implies that in the course of the sixteenth century England became a Protestant country. Given the diversity of religious attitudes outlined in previous chapters we need to consider how appropriate this description is: what does it mean to describe England as Protestant by the end of Elizabeth's reign?

According to the laws of the land, England became a Protestant realm in 1559. This legislative definition of religion was more important than twentieth-century readers may appreciate. The nation-states that emerged in sixteenth-century Europe were validated by religion. People who adhered to alternative faiths in preference to the official one challenged the political as well as the religious order. In England citizenship and creed were inseparable, as they were in most other European states. To be an English person was to be a member of the Church of England. The faith of the national church was, like it or not, the faith of the people of England for few could conceive of religious pluralism in society. Local parish churches, the primary focus of many people's religious loyalty, bore royal coats-of-arms and were the setting for a Protestant liturgy. The growth of xenophobic anti-popery reinforced the link between patriotism and Protestant churchmanship. As Elizabeth's reign progressed, Protestantism became a crucial component of national identity, part of what it meant to be English.

The English may increasingly have thought of themselves as a Protestant people, but only a minority accepted – or even understood – the details of Protestant dogma. Rather than relying upon Christ's love alone to put them right with God, most people probably continued to assume that if they were good they would eventually go to heaven. The idea that salvation depended on moral conduct recurred in many popular publications. An almanac published in 1590 affirmed that a "virtuous life doth purchase grace", a concept that would have appalled any theologically literate Protestant (quoted, Capp 1979: 149). But if the population at large failed to grasp the idea that God's acceptance could not be earned, there is evidence that other reformed notions had some impact on how people perceived the world. The religious sentiments reflected in cheap prints may not have been "thoroughly Protestant" but they were, in Tessa Watt's helpful phrase, "distinctly post-Reformation" (Watt 1991: 327). Rather than using doctrinal criteria to assess the degree to which England had become Protestant, it is more helpful to think in terms of a religious spectrum. The modifications in traditional piety which occurred in the course of the sixteenth century meant that English belief and practice moved some way along that spectrum from Catholicism towards Protestantism. The disappearance of the huge industry of prayers for the dead, the demotion of saints and the greater prominence accorded to biblical figures and modern martyrs, the replacement of holy day processions by market day sermons and the use of biblical verses as wall decorations were all signs of a new age. A limited number of people internalized Protestant dogma, but a shift in religious emphasis can be identified both within the church and in the wider religious environment outside.

In 1558 Elizabeth inherited a realm that was still essentially Catholic although it contained vigorous Protestant enclaves. Had she died, as some feared she might, of an illness early in her reign, the nation could probably have reverted to Catholicism, as it did under Mary, with relative ease – albeit at considerable local expense. During the first decades of her rule, Elizabeth's officials were concerned to do away with indicted rites, roods, images and altars, and to enforce the new Protestant order. Thereafter attention focused upon Protestant as much as Catholic challenges to the 1559 settlement, upon the various attempts by Puritans to introduce further reform into the church. When Elizabeth died in 1603 she passed on to her successor a land in which Protestantism was the acknowledged faith although a fairly quiescent Catholic presence remained. The religious battles that were to tear England apart in the first half of the seventeenth century were to be fought not between Catholics and Protestants but between different brands of Protestant. That shows the extent to which England had moved in a Protestant direction in the course of Elizabeth's reign.

Select bibliography

The content of the works listed below is frequently indicated in the title. In some cases an additional note has been provided to help students identify relevant texts for further reading.

Aston, M. *Lollards and reformers: images and literacy in late medieval religion*. London: Hambledon Press, 1984.

Barry, J. Literacy and literature in popular culture: reading and writing in historical perspective. In *Popular culture in England* c.*1500–1830*, T. Harris (ed.). Basingstoke: Macmillan, 1995.

Bossy, J. *The English Catholic community 1570–1850*. London: Dartman, Longman & Todd, 1975.

Bossy, J. *Christianity in the West 1400–1700*. Oxford: Oxford University Press, 1985. Outlines how pre-Reformation Catholics thought and the religious consequences of the Reformation.

Boulton, J. The limits of formal religion: the administration of Holy Communion in late Elizabethan and early Stuart England. *London Journal* 10, pp. 135–54, 1984. Includes consideration of the number of people attending communion.

Bowker, M. *The Henrician Reformation, the diocese of Lincoln . . . 1521–1547*. Cambridge: Cambridge University Press, 1981. Examines responses to early reforms in a large diocese.

Brigden, S. Youth and the English Reformation. *Past and Present* 95, pp. 37–67, 1982.

Brigden, S. *London and the Reformation*. Oxford: Clarendon Press, 1989.

Burke, P. *Popular culture in early modern Europe*. London: T. Smith, 1978. The first major study of popular culture; includes chapters on the world of carnival and the reform of popular culture.

Capp, B. *Astrology and the popular press: English almanacs 1500–1800*. London: Faber & Faber, 1979.

Clark, P. *English provincial society from the Reformation to the revolution: Kent 1500–1640*. Hassocks: Harvester Press, 1977.

Clark, S. Inversion, misrule and the meaning of witchcraft. *Past and Present* 87, pp. 98–127, 1980. Explains how belief in witchcraft made sense in a society which thought in terms of antitheses.

Clark, S. Protestant demonology: sin, superstition and society (c. 1520–c. 1630). In *Early modern European witchcraft*, B. Ankarloo & G. Henningsen (eds). Oxford: Clarendon Press, 1990. Describes Protestant pastors' responses to witchcraft.

Collinson, P. *The Elizabethan Puritan movement*. London: Jonathan Cape, 1967.

Collinson, P. *The religion of the Protestants*. Oxford: Clarendon Press, 1982. Essays on various aspects of church life, including analyses of popular and unpopular religion and semi-separatist Puritan tendencies.

Collinson, P. *Godly people*. London: Hambledon Press, 1983. Includes essays on popular and unpopular religion and sabbatarianism.

Collinson, P. The Elizabethan church and the new religion. In *The reign of Elizabeth I*, C. Haigh (ed.). Basingstoke: Macmillan, 1984. Concise evocation of Elizabethan Protestantism.

Collinson, P. *The birthpangs of Protestant England*. Basingstoke: Macmillan, 1988. Examines nature of Protestant nation, town and family, and changing Protestant attitude to art and drama.

Collinson, P. Shepherds, sheepdogs and hirelings: the pastoral ministry in post-Reformation England. In *The ministry: clerical and lay*, W. J. Sheils & D. Wood (eds). Oxford: Blackwell, 1989.

Collinson, P. The late medieval church and its Reformation (1400–1600). In *The Oxford illustrated history of Christianity*, J. McManners (ed.). Oxford: Oxford University Press, 1990. Brief survey of ways in which European Christianity changed.

Cressy, D. *Bonfires and bells: national memory and the Protestant calendar in Elizabethan and Stuart England*. London: Weidenfeld & Nicholson, 1989. Explores emergence of new secular, dynastic calendar alongside old religious one.

Cressy, D. Purification, thanksgiving and the churching of women in post-Reformation England. *Past and Present* 141, pp. 106–46, 1993. Examines different meanings people gave to ceremony of churching women.

Cross, C. *Church and people 1450–1660: the triumph of the laity in the English church*. Glasgow: Fontana, 1976.

Cross, C. Parochial structure and the dissemination of Protestantism in sixteenth-century England: a tale of two cities. In *The church in town and countryside*, D. Baker (ed.). Oxford: Blackwell, 1979. Explains why reformed views spread more quickly in Hull than in York.

Dickens, A. G. *Lollards and Protestants in the diocese of York 1509–1558*.

London: Oxford University Press, 1959.

Dickens, A. G. *The English Reformation*, new edn. London: Batsford, 1989. The classic account of the English Reformation, now updated.

Dickens, A. G. The early expansion of Protestantism in England. In *Reformation to revolution*, M. Todd (ed.). London: Routledge, 1995. Reprinted from *Archiv für Reformationsgeschichte* 79, 1988. Presents arguments for early dissemination of Protestantism.

Doran, S. & C. Durston *Princes, pastors and people: the church and religion in England 1529–1689*. London: Routledge, 1991. Thematic survey of major religious changes.

Duffy, E. *The stripping of the altars: traditional religion in England 1400–1580*. New Haven and London: Yale University Press, 1992. Evokes appeal of pre-Reformation Catholicism.

Durston, C. & J. Eales (eds) *The culture of English Puritanism 1560–1700*. Basingstoke: Macmillan, 1996. Provides introduction to Puritanism, examines it as a form of popular culture, and explores Puritan attitudes to church courts, images, and death.

Gee H. & W. J. Hardy (eds) *Documents illustrative of English church history*. London: Macmillan, 1910.

Godbeer, R. *The devil's dominion, magic and religion in early New England*. Cambridge: Cambridge University Press, 1992. Illustrates intertwining of religion and magic in a Puritan society.

Goring, J. *Godly exercises or the devil's dance: Puritanism and popular culture in pre-civil war England*. London: Dr Williams's Trust, 1983.

Green, I. "For Children in Yeares and Children in Understanding": the emergence of the English catechism under Elizabeth and the early Stuarts. *Journal of Ecclesiastical History* 37, pp. 397–425, 1986.

Haigh, C. *Reformation and resistance in Tudor Lancashire*. London: Cambridge University Press, 1975. Account of a region in which Protestantism made slow headway.

Haigh, C. The Church of England, the Catholics and the people. In *The reign of Elizabeth I*, C. Haigh (ed.). Basingstoke: Macmillan, 1984. Stresses failure of both Catholic and Protestant missionaries; introduces concept of "parish Anglicanism".

Haigh, C. (ed.) *The English Reformation revised*. Cambridge: Cambridge University Press, 1987. Selection of revisionist essays, challenging Dickens' interpretation of the Reformation.

Haigh, C. *English Reformations*. Oxford: Clarendon Press, 1993. History of religious changes differentiating legislative reformations from a very partial popular Reformation.

Hall, D. *Worlds of wonder, days of judgment: popular religious belief in early New England*. Cambridge, Mass: Harvard University Press, 1990. Illustrates varied sources of supernaturalist belief in a Puritan society.

Hanawalt, B. *The ties that bound: peasant families in medieval England*. Oxford: Oxford University Press, 1986. Includes discussion of guild as surrogate family.

Heal F. & R. O'Day (eds) *Church and society in England: Henry VIII to James I*. Basingstoke: Macmillan, 1977. Includes essays on popular reactions to Reformation, its impact on popular culture and religion in provincial towns.

Houlbrooke, R. *Church courts and the people during the English Reformation 1520–1570*. Oxford: Oxford University Press, 1979.

Hutton, R. *The rise and fall of merry England: the ritual year 1400–1700*. Oxford: Oxford University Press, 1994.

Hutton, R. The English Reformation and the evidence of folklore. *Past and Present* 148, pp. 89–116, 1995. Uses folklore evidence to show how old practices continued but lost religious meaning.

Ingram, M. Ridings, rough music and the "reform of popular culture" in early modern England. *Past and Present* 105, pp. 79–113, 1984. Argues that there was not a stark divide between popular and elite culture.

Ingram, M. *Church courts, sex and marriage in England 1570–1640*. Cambridge: Cambridge University Press, 1987. Includes chapter on religion and the people.

Ingram, M. From Reformation to toleration: popular religious culture in England 1540–1690. In *Popular culture in England c. 1500–1830*, T. Harris (ed.). Basingstoke: Macmillan, 1995.

Kitch, M. J. The Reformation in Sussex. In *Studies in Sussex Church History*, M. J. Kitch (ed.). London: Leopard's Head Press, 1981.

Lake, P. Anti-popery: the structure of a prejudice. In *Conflict in early Stuart England*, R. Cust & A. Hughes (eds). London: Longman, 1989. Although focusing on Stuart period throws light on earlier anti-Catholicism.

Lake, P. Deeds against nature: cheap print, Protestantism and murder in early seventeenth-century England. In *Culture and politics in early Stuart England*, K. Sharpe & P. Lake (eds). Basingstoke: Macmillan, 1994. Examines religious attitudes revealed in popular murder pamphlets.

Loades, D. The origins of English Protestant nationalism. In *Religion and national identity*, S. Mews (ed.). Oxford: Blackwell, 1982.

MacCulloch, D. *Suffolk and the Tudors: politics and religion in an English county 1500–1600*. Oxford: Clarendon Press, 1986.

MacCulloch, D. *The later Reformation in England 1547–1603*. Basingstoke: Macmillan, 1990. Concise outline of legislative and theological changes and popular responses to them.

MacCulloch, D. *Building a godly realm: the establishment of English Protestantism 1558–1603*. London: Historical Association, 1992.

Macfarlane, A. *Witchcraft in Tudor and Stuart England*. London: Routledge & Kegan Paul, 1970.

Maltby, J. *Approaches to the study of religious conformity in late Elizabethan and early Stuart England: with special reference to Cheshire and the diocese of Lincoln.* PhD thesis, Faculty of History, University of Cambridge, 1991.

Maltby, J. "By this book": parishioners, the prayer book and the established church. In *The early Stuart church*, K. Fincham (ed.). Basingstoke: Macmillan, 1993. Provides evidence for existence of Prayer Book Protestants.

Marsh, C. W. *The Family of Love in English society 1550–1630.* Cambridge: Cambridge University Press, 1994. Detailed examination of a mystical sect.

O'Day, R. *The debate on the English Reformation.* London: Methuen, 1986. Historiographical account of changing interpretations.

Parker, G. Success and failure during the first century of the Reformation. *Past and Present* 136, pp. 43–82, 1992. European perspective on factors inhibiting spread of Protestant ideas.

Phythian-Adams, C. Ceremony and the citizen: the communal year at Coventry 1450–1550. In *Crisis and order in English towns 1500–1700*, P. Clark & P. Slack (eds). London: Routledge & Kegan Paul, 1972. Detailed outline of religious and secular ceremonial year.

Reay, B. (ed.) *Popular culture in seventeenth-century England.* London: Croom Helm, 1985. Although seventeenth century in focus, chapters on popular religion, literature and rough music are relevant to topics discussed in this book.

Reynolds, S. Social mentalities and the case of medieval scepticism. *Transactions of the Royal Historical Society* 6th Series, 1, pp. 21–41, 1991. Argues that medieval mindset could embrace atheism.

Rosser, G. Parochial conformity and voluntary religion in late medieval England. *Transactions of the Royal Historical Society* 6th Series, 1 pp. 173–89, 1991. Illustrates local religious diversity.

Scarisbrick, J. J. *Henry VIII.* London: Eyre & Spottiswoode, 1968.

Scarisbrick, J. J. *The Reformation and the English people.* Oxford: Blackwell, 1984. An early challenge to the idea that the Reformation was welcomed by the English people; includes study of lay fraternities.

Scribner, R. W. The Reformation, popular magic and the disenchantment of the world. *Journal of Interdisciplinary History* 23, pp. 475–94, 1993. Stresses that European Protestants like Catholics believed in a deeply sacralized world.

Sheils, W. J. Erecting the discipline in provincial England: the order of Northampton 1571. In *Humanism and reform: the church in Europe, England and Scotland 1400–1643*, J. Kirk (ed.). Oxford: Blackwell, 1991. Examination of one attempt to introduce Calvinist discipline.

Sommerville, C. J. *The secularization of early modern England.* Oxford: Oxford University Press, 1992. Argues that Reformation marked shift from universal religious culture to more individualist religious faith.

Spufford, M. Can we count the "godly" and the "conformable" in the seventeenth century? *Journal of Ecclesiastical History* 36, pp. 428–38, 1985. Argues for widespread conformity among ordinary people to Church of England.

Spufford, M. Puritanism and social control. In *Order and disorder in early modern England*, A. Fletcher & J. Stevenson (eds). Cambridge: Cambridge University Press, 1985. Argues that attempts to control sexual behaviour were motivated as much by economics as religion.

Swanson, R. N. *Church and society in late medieval England*. Oxford: Blackwell, 1989. Overview of part religion played in pre-Reformation life.

Swanson, R. N. *Catholic England: faith and observance before the Reformation*. Manchester: Manchester University Press, 1993. Introduction characterizes pre-Reformation Catholicism.

Thomas, K. *Religion and the decline of magic*. London: Weidenfeld & Nicholson, 1971.

Walker, G. Heretical sects in pre-Reformation England. *History Today* 43 (May 1993), pp. 42–48. Argues boundary heresy and orthodoxy blurred.

Wallace, D. D. George Gifford, Puritan propaganda and popular religion in Elizabethan England. *Sixteenth Century Journal* 9, pp. 27–49, 1978. Outlines views of Puritan lecturer and writer.

Walsham, A. *Church Papists*. Woodbridge: Boydell Press, 1993. Examination of Catholics who conformed to Church of England.

Watt, T. *Cheap print and popular piety 1550–1640*. Cambridge: Cambridge University Press, 1991. Uses popular cheap prints to study nature of religious influence on common life.

White, B. R. *The English Separatist tradition*. London: Oxford University Press, 1971. Traces development of those who separated from Church of England.

Whiting, R. *The blind devotion of the people, popular religion and the English Reformation*. Cambridge: Cambridge University Press, 1989. Examines response to religious change in south west.

Wright, S. J. (ed.) *Parish, church and people: local studies in lay religion 1350–1750*. London: Hutchinson, 1988. Includes essays on guilds, purgatory, sixteenth-century parish life in Chester, and post-Reformation attitudes to young people.

Index